The Shape Method for Jazz Improvisation

Malcolm Lynn Baker

"I think that the idea that jazz can be learned by using a harmonic approach, as opposed to a melodic approach, is essentially a flawed philosophy. It's much easier to teach people the harmonic constructs than to force them to learn music by ear, which is far more difficult. One of the problems I have with a lot of today's jazz is the lack of melody and overemphasis on harmonic associations."

Branford Marsalis
Branford Marsalis Frankly Speaking
Marc Chenard, May 30, 2007.
http://www.scena.org/lsm/sm12-8/sm12-8_marsalis_en.html

Cover art *Oranges* by Kalin Baker. © 2014, www.kalinartandspirit.com

Copyright © 2011-2014 by Malcor Music Publishing

All rights reserved. Printed in the United States of America. This publication is protected by Copyright and permission should be obtained from the publisher prior to any prohibited reproduction, storage in a retrieval system, or transmission in any form or by any means, electronic mechanical, photocopying, recording, or likewise. To obtain permissions(s) to use material from this work, please submit a written request to Malcor Music Publishing, 4485 @ 61st Place, Arvada, CO 80003.

Table of Contents

Preface i

Introduction to *The Shape Method* iii

1. The Charleston Rhythm, 1st Order Major and Minor Consonance Tones and Phrasing 1

2. Displaced Charleston Rhythm and Chromatic 1st Degree Resolutions 11

3. Phrase Ending Rhythms and Chromatic 2nd Degree Resolutions 17

4. Eighth-Note Rhythms Embedded in the Charleston Rhythm and 1st Degree Suspensions 23

5. Motivic Development Through Displacement and Sequence and Interpreting Half-Diminished Chords 29

6. Using Triplets and Triplet Avoid and Rhythms and Bi-Directional Resolutions 33

7. Anticipations and 2nd Order Consonances and Diminished Chords 39

8. Varying Rhythmic Values and Anchor Phrases 45

9. Multiple Pickup Notes and Direction Change Device – Ornamentation 49

10. Multiple Syncopations and Direction Change Device - Desc. To Asc. & Asc. To Desc. 57

11. Micro-Resolutions with Triplets and Direction Change Device - Octave Displacement 61

12. Adjusting Harmonic Rhythm for Slow Tempos and Direction Change Device - Suspension Escape Tones 65

13. Adjusting Harmonic Rhythm for Fast Tempos and Direction Change Device - Consonance Escape Tones 69

14. Micro-Resolutions with Sixteenths and Extended Bi-Directional Resolutions 73

15. Re-Barring and Harmonic Rhythm - Delay and Anticipation 77

16. The Son and Rumba Clave and Super-Impositions on Minor and Major Triads 83

17. Playing In Clave and Super-Impositions on Dominant Chords I 89

18. Cross-Metering I and Super-Impositions on Dominant Chords II 95

19. Cross-Metering II and Shape Stealing 101

20. Mixed Meter Clave and 3rd Order Consonances 107

21. Metric Modulation I and Extracting Quartal Materials from Super-Impositions 117

22. Metric Modulation II and Diminished Four Tonic System 123

23. Motivic Development Through Augmentation and Diminution and Augmented and Whole Tone Three and Six Tonic Systems 130

Glossary of Terms .... a

Appendix I – Advanced Chord Implications of Chromatic Super-Impositions .... d

Appendix II – Why The Blues Scale Works .... f

Appendix III – Public Domain Jazz Phrases with Shape Method Analysis .... k

The Shape Method for Jazz Improvisation
Lynn Baker

Preface

The Shape Method developed from years of experience teaching jazz improvisation. In those years I have noticed that the various methods employed were not as successful as I thought they should be.

For a long time I thought that student listening habits, perhaps not focused on jazz as much as they should be, were a major contributor to the problem. Jazz is an aural language, and it is widely acknowledged that listening to it is crucial to being able to play it. However, I have had many experiences with students who I know are listening a lot but still not able to play in a convincing jazz style.

I have also worked with very intelligent students, who thoroughly understand one of the major tenets of existing jazz improvisation pedagogy – chord/scale relationships. They have practiced the scales and arpeggios and are able to provide the "correct" materials on demand. And yet, they too frequently have problems improvising in a convincing jazz style.

Students who have great ears also sometimes have difficulty playing in a convincing jazz style. They have transcribed, memorized, and performed solos from major improvisers, sometimes at a remarkable level of technical accomplishment – and yet…

And there are students who have studiously analyzed improvisations and adapted the best language of the improvisers. They carefully learn the phrases, transpose them, and then place them in exactly the correct locations in a written solo. Then, they learn their compositions and are able to play them – but when asked to improvise are unable to transition their knowledge into an artistic statement in a jazz style.

It seems to me the reason for these myriad failures is an absence of foundational principles of bebop jazz improvisation from texts or methods - texts and methods that focused almost exclusively on harmony to the exclusion of other important aspects of jazz improvisation.

I believe this chord/scale-centered pedagogy developed because the first two generations of jazz educators were schooled in Western Art Music Theory. "Classical" theory spends months of class time on harmonic analysis issues, rarely addressing rhythmic concerns and never covering expressive devices in a rigorous, analytical way. Therefore, the first two generations of jazz educators had good tools with which to adapt their knowledge of harmony to the practice of jazz improvisation but very little framework with which to create a pedagogy that deals with other, extremely crucial, elements of jazz improvisation.

In short, I believe the missing elements from existing pedagogy are a course on Rhythmic and Melodic Shape in jazz improvisation. This book is an attempt to develop such a pedagogy.

Acknowledgements

I'd like to thank the following scholars, performers, composers, and educators for their extremely valuable work: David N. Baker, Jamey Aebersold, Ramon Ricker, Hal Galper, George Russell, Jerry Coker, Gary Campbell, James Casale, Jerry Greene, Rebeca Mauleon, John Santos, Richard Boukas, and Antonio Garcia. Their foundational work in jazz improvisation and folkloric pedagogy has made this work possible. I'd also like to thank the decades of students who have worked with me to try to learn this majestic art form.

The Shape Method for Jazz Improvisation
Lynn Baker

INTRODUCTION

The Shape Method is focused on ways to develop excellent jazz solos through concepts of melodic and rhythmic shape. However, there are additional foundational skills and knowledge that are important and those ideas are briefly discussed here.

I began this project by trying to distill years of listening to great jazz improvisations down to their common, foundational characteristics. I was trying to answer the question, "What makes a great jazz improvisation?"

After considering the question for a number of years, I was able to isolate what I believe are the crucial elements that are common to all great jazz improvisations. Upon identifying the various parts, their priority and relationships became obvious to me.

Therefore, below is my proposal of an appropriate hierarchy for teaching jazz improvisation.
1) Jazz Tone
2) Jazz Time
3) Jazz Rhythm
4) Jazz Shape
5) Jazz Pitches

JAZZ TONE

Core Tone

The ability of the player to make what I call a great "Core Tone" is the absolute necessity for becoming a successful jazz improviser. Core Tone is no different in jazz than any other good sound on your instrument and is defined by two elements:

1) <u>Consistent support</u> of the sound, however the sound is generated; breath, bow speed and pressure, etc.

2) <u>Beautiful resonance</u> of the tone throughout the instrument and, in fact, the performer.

Without these two attributes, a good jazz tone cannot be achieved. However, that is only the beginning of a good jazz tone.

The Shape Method - Introduction

Articulation and Expressive Devices

Most of the character of the sound of any instrument is determined by the quality of the articulation. In fact, many times it is very difficult to discern one instrument from another when the articulation is removed. A good jazz tone depends even more on the character of the articulation.

Why? because articulation in jazz is a principle expressive gesture and there is a broad palette from which to draw. In addition, many notes in jazz have articulations at the end of the note and this adds another element of expression and rhythmic energy. The added rhythmic energy provided by articulations at the end of notes is a vital component of Jazz Tone and Jazz Time.

The following chart addresses various expressive devices, including articulations. These devices should be available for an improviser to use as the musical moment allows, based on considerations of style, tempo, and mood.

At Beginning of the Note	After the Note has Begun	At the End of the Note
Hard Articulation	Crescendo	Hard Articulation
Breath Articulation	Diminuendo	Lift
Half-Tongue Articulation	Add Vibrato	Fade
Quick Scoop	Remove Vibrato	Short/Long Fall
Long Scoop	Make Vibrato Wider/More Shallow	Fingered Fall
Rip Down	Make Vibrato Faster/Slower	"Squeeze" Fall
Rip Up	Move to/from Multiphonic	Breath Fall
Splat	Trills	Doit Up

These and other expressive devices are key elements of good Jazz Tone and their application should be studied in the music of the master improvisers and emulated.

JAZZ TIME

There is an interesting, and seemingly contradictory set of conditions at the heart of what I call "Jazz Time." Jazz Time is steady, but not obvious.

Jazz Pulse

One of the reasons it is not obvious is that the essential pulse character of jazz is <u>legato</u>. That does not mean there are no accents or short notes in jazz. On the contrary, it means that the accented and short notes have additional meaning because they are framed and supported by the legato environment. The legato pulse environment is accomplished principally through two instruments:

1) The Bass playing on each beat of the measure in a very connected style.

2) The Ride Cymbal which generates a very connected sound due to its ringing character.

In common meter, jazz time is felt on one and three, the beats where the harmonic movement occurs. It is crucial to maintain a steady pulse with natural <u>unaccented</u> pulses on one and three before one can move to the next element of jazz time – syncopation.

In other meters, jazz time continues to be felt on the strong beats. For example: in ¾ meter jazz time is felt on 1, in 5/8 meter jazz time is felt either on 1 and 4 or 1 and 3, depending on whether it is a 3+2 or 2+3 division of the pulse. Similar pulse groupings are the foundation of jazz time in all other meters.

Basic Jazz Syncopation

The most basic syncopation in common-time jazz is the accent on two and four. This contrast of an accented "up" on two and four, to the harmonic rhythm's "down" on one and three is what generates the "lilting" feeling of jazz. This is why it is so crucial to be able to hold a steady pulse on one and three before moving to the jazz syncopation feel of two and four.

When dividing the beat, higher math skills are needed because each beat needs to be divided into three equal parts – yes, triplets are the jazz division. Rarely are all three notes of the triplet played, usually notes are played on only the first and third triplets.

Jazz Time Articulation

The articulation comes into play here to generate phrases in good jazz time. When playing steady eighth-notes the articulation on the downbeat note is long, consumes two triplet values and is <u>without</u> an articulation at the end of the note. The note on the final triplet is also long and articulated, and is slightly accented at the beginning of the note (for wind instruments <u>with the breath</u>, not a hard tongue). The end of the second note is also unarticulated.

In this series of "eight-notes" the last note of the triplet is slurred to the downbeat note. This generates a series of uneven yet legato swung eighth-notes that have slight accents off the beat.

The next three elements of the Hierarchy; Jazz Rhythm, Shape, and Pitches, are addressed systematically through the course of the text.

How The Shape Method is Organized

Each chapter contains at least two concepts, a rhythmic idea and a pitch-related concept. At the intersection of rhythm and pitch is Shape, the focus of this text. There is a written explanation of the idea and examples of its use. At the conclusion of each chapter are suggested listening examples and a set of exercises designed to give readers experience with the concepts. There are two types of exercises; composition and performance. The goal of the composition exercises is for the student to develop their personal language within the Bebop style and therefore should also be learned and performed.

It should also be noted that the organization is cumulative and concepts covered in earlier chapters should be retained and continue to be applied as more advanced concepts are learned.

Conclusion

The Shape Method is presented as a way to gain a holistic understanding and practice of Bebop jazz improvisation. It is NOT a substitute for the established jazz improvisation pedagogy. While I employ the Shape Method as the central focus of my jazz improvisation teaching I continue to teach chord/scale relationships, tune learning, "lick" transposition and application, solo transcription and analysis, and a historical understanding of the music. Gaining command of these foundational skills and knowledge is necessary to be able to apply the lessons of shape discussed in this text.

Chapter 1 – The Charleston Rhythm, 1st Order Major and Minor Consonance Tones and Phrasing

The Charleston Rhythm

The heart of jazz rhythm is the "Charleston" rhythm and its variations. The "Charleston" is from the famous rag by J.P. Johnson of the same name, but its origins are African and Afro-Cuban. It began as a variation of a bell pattern from Africa.

AFRICAN BELL PATTERN

The articulations at the ends of the measures were removed resulting in a Clave rhythm.

"3-2" CLAVE

The second, two-articulation measure of the rhythm was dropped and the third articulation was removed from the three-articulation measure.

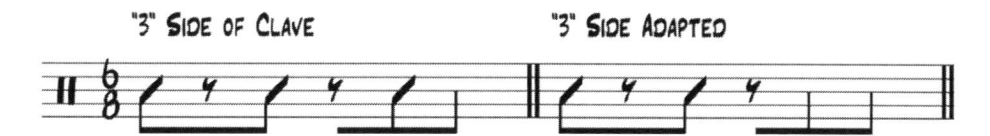

"3" SIDE OF CLAVE   *"3" SIDE ADAPTED*

The result is the "Proto-Charleston" rhythm. Lengthening the second note of the rhythm creates the Charleston rhythm. Please note, the dotted-quarter pulse of the 6/8 meter is equal to the half-note of the 4/4 Swing meter, providing the rhythmic equivalence.

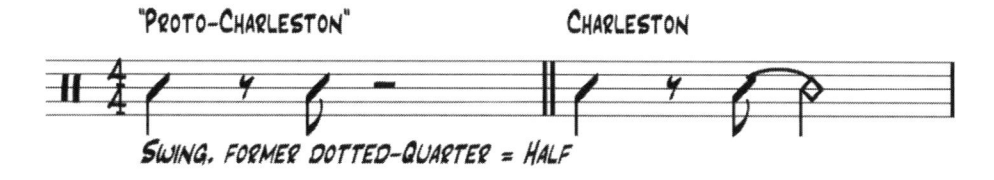

"PROTO-CHARLESTON"   *CHARLESTON*
SWING, FORMER DOTTED-QUARTER = HALF

In its native jazz form the Charleston Rhythm consists of a short note on one and a long note on the & of two. Say the phrase "Charles-ton," with an accent on the "ton," to get the feeling of the phrase. Keep in mind that the triplet division permeates these rhythms and all notes occurring on the "&" of the beat are actually on a triplet division of the pulse.

The Shape Method – Chapter 1

The two common forms of the Charleston Rhythm are length variations of the original phrase:

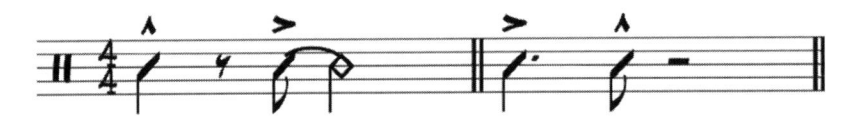

With the exception of extremely slow tempos, the off-beat note of the Charleston Rhythm is not performed on the last triplet division of the quarter-note pulse.

Rather, because of the rhythmic shift from dotted-quarter pulse to half-note pulse, it is within the triplet division of the half-note pulse. And here is where jazz gets its swing, there is a three-against-two rhythmic tension created between the steady quarter-note of the bass walking on each beat, and the half-note triplet of the Charleston Rhythm. Trombonist Wayne Wallace says this tension is the heart of swing. The examples below illustrate this rhythmic tension.

The first step is to re-conceptualize the "3" Side of the Clave from 6/8 to 6/4. Remember the Adapted "3" Side is the basis of the Charleston Rhythm. Here are the originals.

Now, the same rhythm with the underlying pulse value doubled from eighth-note to quarter-note so the three-against-two tension can be seen more clearly.

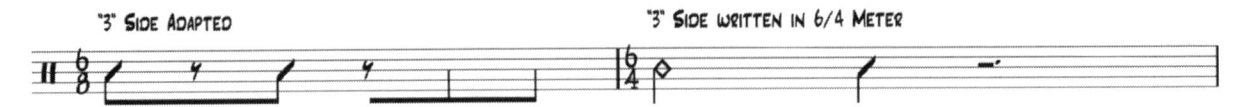

In the final example the Charleston Rhythm, written in 6/4 so the pulse unit is consistent with 4/4 jazz meter, is on the top line, the underlying 4/4 walking bass pulse is on the second line, and the triplet subdivision of the walking bass pulse is on the bottom line. This example clearly demonstrates exactly where the second articulation of the Charleston Rhythm occurs in 4/4 jazz time.

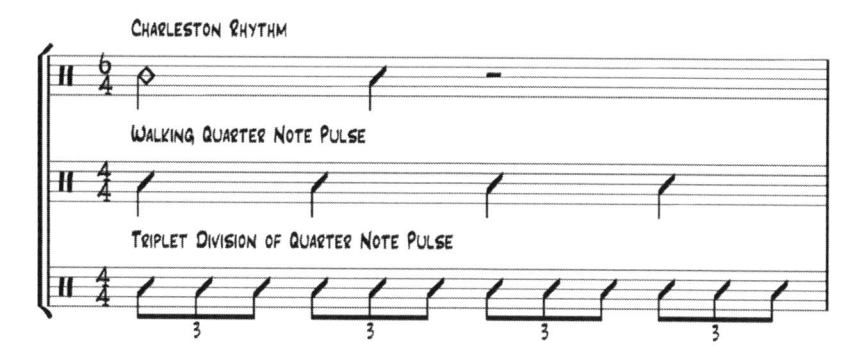

Of course, as the Charleston Rhythm is rhythmically displaced (as in Chapter 2) this underlying tension needs to be maintained to give the figures their swing feel.

Consonance Tones

When beginning to think about pitches to choose to construct a melody it is important to identify the resting sounds within the chord. Understanding on which pitches the melody can come to rest allows the improviser to control tension and release, and construct more appealing melodies.

The Shape Method addresses chord tones through three sets of triads referred to as the 1st, 2nd, and 3rd Order Triads. The 1st Order triad is built from the Root of the chord, the 2nd Order, built from the Fifth, and the 3rd Order from the Ninth. The following discussion of Consonance Tones refers to 1st Order triads.

The Shape Method defines the resting points of a chord as Consonance Tones. In Major and Minor chords the following are Consonance Tones: The Root, Third, the Fifth, and Major Sixth. These are Consonance Tones regardless of the quality of any chord tone past the triad (meaning the qualities of the 2nd and 3rd Order triads). 2nd and 3rd Order Triads contain no Consonance Tones until the harmonic rhythm is very slow, e.g., modal jazz.

For minor chords, the Fourth is also a Consonance Tone. In the case of Dominant Chords the Fifth, when not sustained, is a Consonance Tone if it is Diminished, Perfect, or Augmented.

The chart below displays the Consonance Tones of the 1st Order.

Chord Quality	Root	Third	Fourth	Fifth	Sixth
Major	Yes	Major		Perfect	Major
Minor	Yes	Minor	Perfect	Perfect	Major
Dominant	Yes	Major		Diminished, Perfect, or Augmented	Major

Melodic Direction

Melodic direction is a crucial concept of the Shape Method. Melodic direction is addressed by placing almost every note in context with those that precede or follow. The next section defines melodic direction in the Shape Method.

Strong Beats

The concept of **Strong Beats** in jazz needs to be defined before discussing melodic direction. Harmonies are stated on the strong beats of the measure, in 4/4 time those beats are 1 and 3, in 3/4 the strong beat is 1. Chords change on these beats and therefore are the foundation of all syncopation and melodic tension and release. In a vast majority of cases, Consonance Tones are associated with Strong Beats. Non-Consonance tones that occur off of Strong Beats are defined as Resolution Tones.

Types of Melodic Direction

There are obviously three types of melodic direction; static, ascending, and descending. The Shape Method defines ascending melodic direction as **Drive**. The implication is the melody has a strong motion to achieve a higher pitch. **Gravity** is the term applied to descending melodic direction and implies the melody pulling down to a lower pitch. These terms are not chosen lightly and are intended to convey a sense of activity and purpose to the melodic direction – a key element in good melodic construction.

Resolution Tones

The Shape Method frequently refers to Drive and Gravity through devices called Resolutions. Resolutions are identified in two ways; direction and length. Regardless of these factors, Resolutions have two identifying characteristics:

1) They are <u>never</u> further than a whole step away from the next pitch, AND

2) They are <u>always</u> identified in the context of what direction they are <u>going</u>.

The basic concept is that a **Drive Resolution** is a note that is <u>beneath</u> the next Consonance Tone, and a **Gravity Resolution** is a note that is <u>above</u> the next Consonance Tone.

Resolutions are described by their length; how many consecutive non-Consonance tones precede a Consonance tone. **1st Degree Resolutions** consist of one note and **2nd Degree Resolutions** of two notes. There are complex combinations of pitches that result in longer resolutions that will be covered later in the Method.

Because Resolution Tones are always contextualized by <u>where they are going</u>, they are considered **Diatonic** when they are notes from <u>the key to which they resolve</u>. For major chords, the major scale represents diatonic materials. For minor chords the Melodic Minor is considered diatonic. Notes outside the associated key areas (e.g., A Flat in C major, or E natural on C minor) are considered **Chromatic** Resolution Tones.

Whereas Resolutions are always identified by the context of where they are <u>going</u>, Consonance Tones are defined by where they are <u>coming from</u>, or the note(s) that **precede**. Therefore, there are three types of Consonance Tones; Consonance Tones that begin phrases or immediately repeat a Consonance Tone are called Consonance Tones, Consonance Tones that are preceded by a note that is higher are called Consonance Gravity tones, and those preceded by a lower note are Consonance Drive tones.

The Shape Method – Chapter 1

The chart below lists the tones, their definitions, and provides their abbreviations.

Name	Definition	Abbreviation
Consonance Tone	A pitch of rest as the first note of the phrase or that directly repeats a previous Consonance Tone.	CT
Consonance Drive Tone	A pitch of rest that is approached from below.	CD
Consonance Gravity Tone	A pitch of rest that is approached from above.	CG
Drive Resolution (1st Degree)	A non-Consonance tone, occurring off a strong beat, that moves up in step-wise motion to a Consonance tone.	D
Gravity Resolution (1st Degree)	A non-Consonance tone, occurring off a strong beat, that moves down in step-wise motion to a Consonance tone.	G
Drive Resolution (2nd Degree)	Two non-Consonance tones, occurring off a strong beat, that move in step-wise motion up to a Consonance Tone.	D – D
Gravity Resolution (2nd Degree)	Two non-Consonance tones, occurring off a strong beat, that move in step-wise motion down to a Consonance Tone.	G – G

These are the C Major and C Minor Diatonic Drive Resolutions moving to Consonance Drive Tones.

These are the C Major and C Minor Diatonic Gravity Resolutions moving to Consonance Gravity Tones.

The following are examples of common jazz phrases analyzed using the Shape Method.

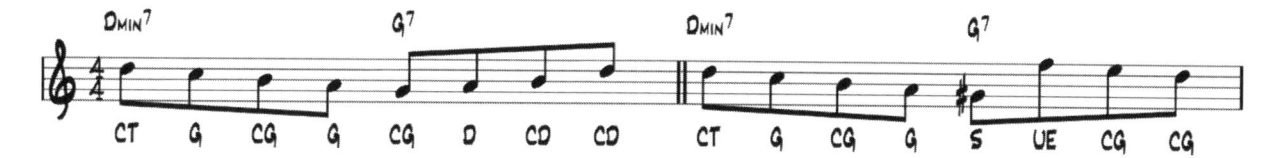

Scales and Arpeggios

The Shape Method is concerned with describing types of melodic shape, and the concepts developed in this book allow for discussion of shape without referring to scales and chord arpeggios. This alternative language allows the Shape Method to move beyond stereotyped concepts of Chord/Scale relationships to discover deeper meanings of melodies. However, scales and arpeggios should be part of the improviser's "tool kit." Its helpful to integrate concepts of Scales and Arpeggios and Shape Method concepts using the following maxim:

Scales are habits of resolution, arpeggios are habits of consonance.

"I dig his phrasing"

"I dig his phrasing" is said all the time but seldom explained. The Shape Method identifies great jazz phrasing as; phrases that start and end in interesting ways and places.

Starting a phrase on the first beat of the form of a tune is not a very interesting place to start, but can be made interesting by the way the phrase is started. As examples, phrase can be made more interesting by beginning with a forte-piano, a splat, a crescendo, a scoop, etc. Or phrases can be made more interesting by varying the places they start by using a 1st Degree Drive or Gravity Resolutions or delaying the start of a phrase. These, and other devices provide interesting places to start phrases.

Phrase Length Variance

In Chapter 9 the Shape Method has a lengthy discussion of phrasing from which concepts of direction change emerge, but there is one feature of that discussion that needs immediate attention. Master improvisers vary the lengths of their phrases.

By playing phrases of different lengths, some long some short, they are able to use this very simple device to create variety, suspense (when will it stop?, when will it start?), and interest.

The Shape Method – Chapter 1

Phrase Endings

In addition to variable phrases lengths, ending phrases off the beat is an effective way to make phrases interesting.

ENDING PHRASES

Short Rhythm   Long Rhythm

Chapter Summary

- The Charleston Rhythm is the foundational rhythm of jazz syncopation and developed from the 6/8 African bell pattern.

- The foundational concepts of the Shape Method were defined.

- Phrasing, especially concerning how and when phrases start and end was discussed.

Suggested Listening

Afternoon In Paris, Blues Walk, I Got Rhythm, Blue Seven

The Shape Method – Chapter 1

EXERCISES

Composition Exercises

When beginning these composition exercises, and any time you are in need of inspiration, it is recommended that you borrow phrases from Appendix II (Why the Blues Scale Works) and III (Public Domain Jazz Phrases with Shape Method Analysis). Remember - jazz is a language, you don't have to invent new words to hold a brilliant conversation.

Each of the melody fragments should have Consonance Tones (CT, CD, or CG) on strong beats. Please analyze and label each pitch with the appropriate Shape Method notation.

1) Write a melody fragment on the following chord changes that:

   a. Begins with a Drive Resolution (it can occur prior to the first chord)

   b. Ends with a short rhythm ending

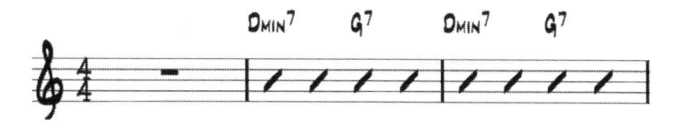

   [Musical staff: 4/4 time, chords: Dmin7, G7, Dmin7, G7]

2) Write a four-measure long melody fragment on the following chord changes that:

   a. Begins with a Charleston Rhythm

   b. Ends with a long rhythm ending

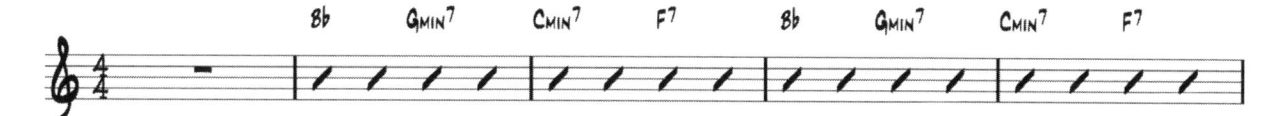

   [Musical staff: 4/4 time, chords: Bb, Gmin7, Cmin7, F7, Bb, Gmin7, Cmin7, F7]

3) Write a three-measure melody fragment on the following chord changes that:

   a. Begins with a Gravity Resolution (it can occur prior to the first chord)

   b. Strings two Charleston Rhythms together immediately

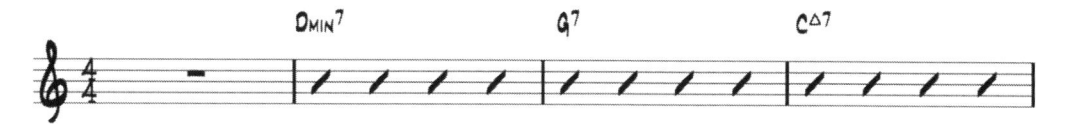

   [Musical staff: 4/4 time, chords: Dmin7, G7, C△7]

Performance Exercise

1) Learn and play Diatonic, 1st Degree Drive and Gravity Resolutions for Major and Minor chords in all keys. (See Etude Supplement, Vol. 1)

Chapter 2 – Displaced Charleston Rhythm and Chromatic Resolution Tones

Displaced Charleston Rhythm

As stated in Chapter 1, the Charleston rhythm is the heart of jazz rhythm. In this chapter we see why that is the case.

Earlier, The Shape Method discussed altering the relationship of "short" and "long" notes of the phrase, creating two versions of the Charleston rhythm.

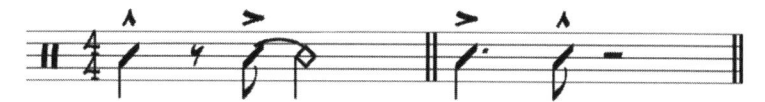

Displacement is another method employed to create rhythmic diversity. When rhythms are displaced, they retain their rhythmic shape - their internal relationships, but they start at a different point in the measure. Rhythmic Displacement of the Charleston Rhythm is used to create many common jazz rhythms.

There are a total of thirteen variations of the "Charleston" rhythm that are commonly used in jazz in 4/4 meter (and two more, rarely used). These variations are created by altering two elements of the original phrase:

1) Reversing the "short" – "long" relationships of the notes

2) Displacing the original rhythm to various locations in the measure

Additional variations can be created by making both notes short or both long, However, these are less common than mixing lengths.

Each variation of the length of the notes is progressively delayed by an eighth-note to provide these fifteen variations.

One measure long variations:

Because these variations cross barlines they are presented in two measure lengths:

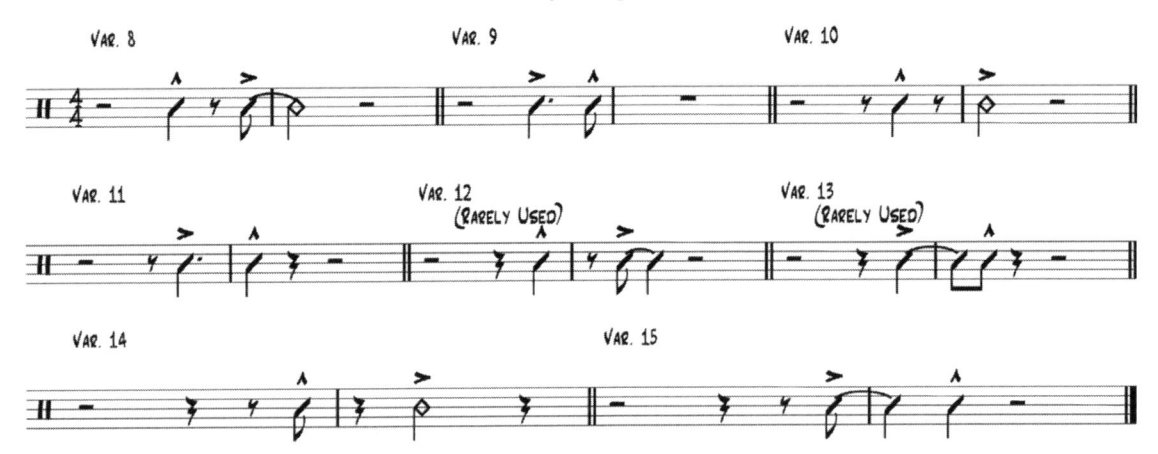

[Musical notation: Var. 8, Var. 9, Var. 10]

[Musical notation: Var. 11, Var. 12 (Rarely Used), Var. 13 (Rarely Used)]

[Musical notation: Var. 14, Var. 15]

Please note that rhythms that begin after an eighth-note rest should be on the second triplet of the strong beat. This is because of their relation to the second measure of the bell pattern rhythm shown below.

[Musical notation: "3-2" Clave]

Rhythm and Harmony

There is a specific association of certain rhythmic shapes and harmony. Notice how the first Charleston rhythm anticipates beat three, the second strong beat of the measure. Many times there are chord changes on beat three and the pitch on that anticipation needs to be associated with the chord on beat three. Moreover, even if the anticipated note is not tied to beat three, the pitch still needs to be associated with the chord – unless there is a note on beat three. In addition, these "rules" should be applied to all strong beats.

It can be confusing, but this "If-Then" table clarifies the relationships:

If the Rhythm	**then** the Pitch
is tied to a Strong Beat	is from Strong Beat Chord.
anticipates a Strong Beat, with no note on the anticipated Strong Beat	is from Strong Beat Chord.
is before a Strong Beat with a note on the Strong Beat	May be a Resolution Tone or a Consonance Tone of the Chord on the Weak Beat.

The Shape Method – Chapter 2

Chromatic Resolution Tones

In Chapter 1 the Shape Method defines Diatonic Resolution Tones as pitches associated with the chord to which they are resolving. Diatonic Resolution Tones for Major chord are from the major scale and Minor are from the Melodic Minor. In this chapter, Chromatic Resolution Tones are defined.

The definition is as clear as it seems, Chromatic Resolution Tones are not from the Major or Melodic Minor scale of the chord to which they are resolving. However, all other definitions apply:

1) They are never further than a whole step away from the next pitch, AND

2) They are always identified in the context of what direction they are going.

Length descriptions, Drive and Gravity, continue to apply to Chromatic Resolution Tones as they did to Diatonic. Chromatic Resolution Tones are noted in analysis as "**D**" Drive or "**G**" Gravity.

These are the C Major and C Minor Chromatic Drive Resolutions moving to Consonance Drive Tones.

These are the C Major and C Minor Chromatic Gravity Resolutions moving to Consonance Gravity Tones.

The following are examples of common jazz phrases that incorporate Chromatic Resolution Tones analyzed using the Shape Method.

Chapter Summary

- The Charleston Rhythm is frequently displaced to create many of the rhythms of jazz.

- The Note before a strong beat can have different harmonic associations, depending upon what happens on the next strong beat.

- Resolution Tones that are <u>outside</u> of the key area to which they are resolving are called Chromatic Resolution Tones.

Suggested Listening

Billie's Bounce, Anthropology, Sandu, Brownie Speaks

The Shape Method – Chapter 2

EXERCISES

Composition Exercises

Each of the phrases should have Consonance Tones (CT, CD, or CG) on strong beats. Phrases should retain the ending rhythms and phrase length variations from Chapter 1 assignments. Please analyze and label each pitch the with appropriate Shape Method notation.

1) Write a two chorus solo on the following chord changes which has (Required components can always be combined within a phrase):

   a. One phrase that begins with a 1st Degree Chromatic Drive Resolution

   b. One phrase that begins with a 1st Degree Chromatic Gravity Resolution

   c. One phrase that begins with a 1st Degree Diatonic Drive Resolution

   d. One phrase that begins with a 1st Degree Diatonic Gravity Resolution

   e. One phrase that begins with a variation of the Charleston Rhythm

   f. Two phrases using the short rhythm ending

   g. Two phrases using the long rhythm ending

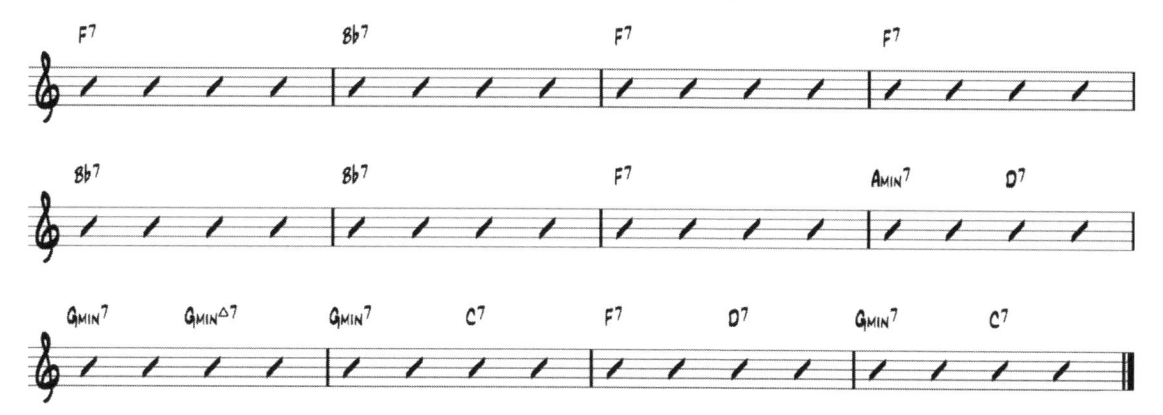

[Chord chart: F7 | Bb7 | F7 | F7 | Bb7 | Bb7 | F7 | Amin7 D7 | Gmin7 Gmin△7 | Gmin7 C7 | F7 D7 | Gmin7 C7]

Performance Exercise

1) Learn and play 1st Degree Chromatic Drive and Gravity Resolutions for Major and Minor chords in all keys. (See Etude Supplement, Vol. 1)

Chapter 3 – Phrase Ending Rhythms and 2nd Degree Resolution Tones

Phrase Ending Rhythms

In Chapter 1 the Short and Long versions of the "& of 1" endings were introduced and their use has been assigned in the composition assignments. Because one of the important components of good phrasing is interesting endings of the phrases, the Shape Method will provide several more ending rhythms.

These rhythms are organized by where they end within the measure, starting early and progressing through the measure. All of these rhythms were transcribed from master improvisers' solo, these are the rhythmic materials used by master musicians Charlie Parker, Bud Powell, Clifford Brown, and others. The notation "Line to…" indicates the presence of melodic materials preceding the phrase ending.

The first examples are the "& of 1" category.

These examples are the "& of 2" category.

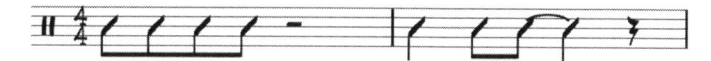

The next demonstrate the "& of 3" category.

These examples are the "& of 4" category.

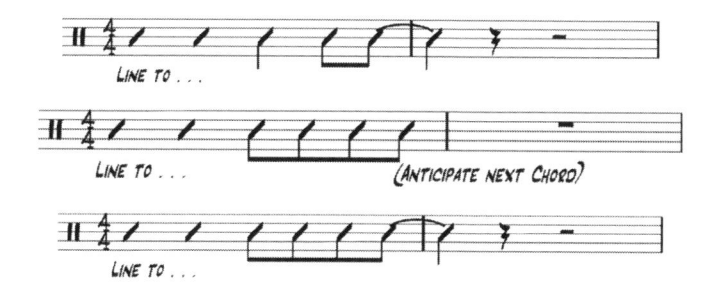

The final examples are the "end on 1" category.

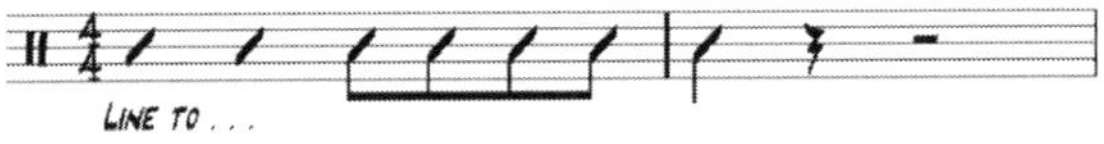

When using these rhythms remember the "Rhythm and Harmony" practice from Chapter 2 concerning the rhythms that anticipate a strong beat.

2nd Degree Resolution Tones

The Shape Method defines **2nd Degree Resolution Tones** as two notes, neither a Consonance tone, moving the same direction – either Gravity or Drive. 2nd Degree Resolutions are notated in analysis with either two "D"s or "G"s with a hyphen between as shown in this common jazz phrase.

All 2nd Degree Resolution Tones involve chromaticism. This is because one of the tones would be a Consonance Tone if it remained in the key.

These are the C Major and C Minor Chromatic Drive Resolutions moving to Consonance Drive Tones.

These are the C Major and C Minor Chromatic Gravity Resolutions moving to Consonance Gravity Tones.

Chapter Summary

- Jazz phrases end in a variety of ways, frequently off the beat and/or in an anticipation.
- 2nd Degree Resolution Tones were defined and it was noted that they all involve chromatic pitches.

Suggested Listening

Oleo, Au Privave, Mohawk, Wee

EXERCISES

Composition Exercises

Each of the phrases should have Consonance Tones (CT, CD, or CG) on strong beats. Phrases should retain variance in length. Please analyze and label each pitch the with appropriate Shape Method notation.

1) Write a solo on the following chord changes which has:

   a. One phrase that begins with a 2nd Degree Chromatic Drive Resolution

   b. One phrase that begins with a 2nd Degree Chromatic Gravity Resolution

   c. One phrase that begins with a 1st Degree Diatonic Drive Resolution

   d. One phrase that begins with a 1st Degree Chromatic Gravity Resolution

   e. One phrase that ends with an "& of 1" category rhythm

   f. One phrase that ends with an "& of 2" category rhythm

   g. One phrase that ends with an "& of 3" category rhythm

   h. One phrase that ends with an "& of 4" category rhythm

   i. One phrase that ends with an "end on 1" category rhythm

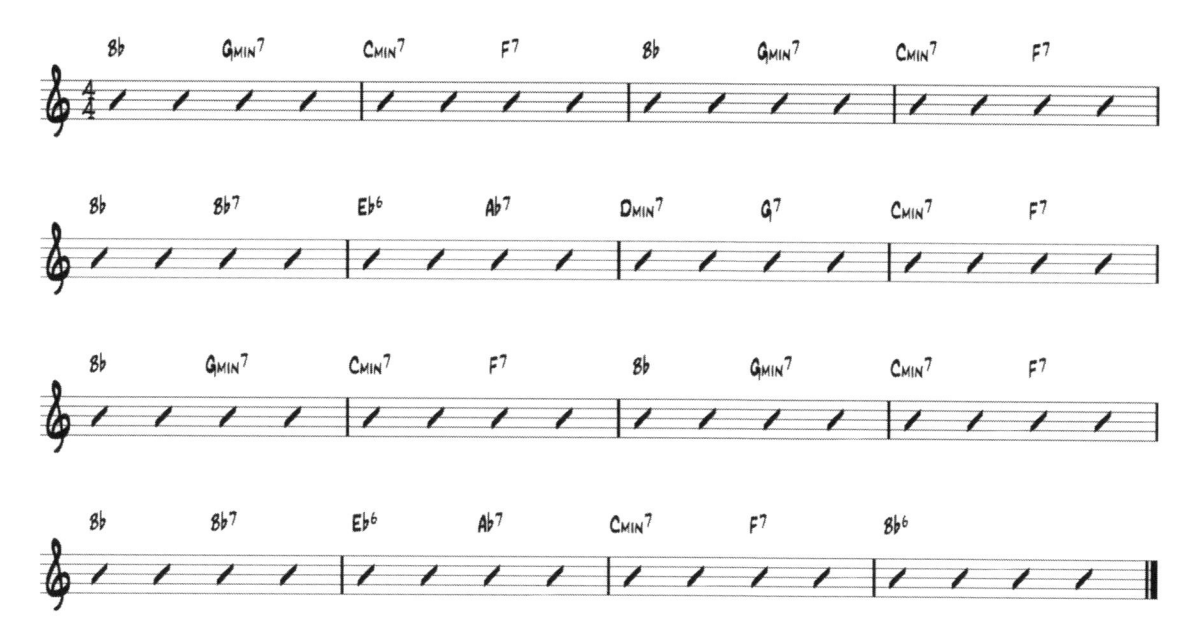

Performance Exercise

1) Learn and play 2nd Degree Chromatic Drive and Gravity Resolutions for Major and Minor chords in all keys. (See Etude Supplement, Vol. 1)

Chapter 4 – Eighth-Note Rhythms Embedded in the Charleston Rhythm and 1st Degree Suspensions

Eighth-Note Rhythms Embedded in the Charleston Rhythm

In the Shape Method, the Charleston Rhythm is the heart of jazz rhythm and even more important is the underlying African and Afro-Cuban pulses from which it comes. In Chapter 1 the Shape Method discussed how the Charleston Rhythm emerged from an African Bell Rhythm. One of the most important concepts is the Triplet rhythm that is implied in the 6/8 Bell pattern and the effect of that pattern on the Charleston Rhythm. While there are subtle "feel" issues of this relationship that the Shape Method will address in later chapters, this chapter will address the eighth-note rhythms embedded in the Charleston and how those can be developed in jazz phrases.

This example demonstrates the four eight-notes that are implied in the Charleston Rhythm.

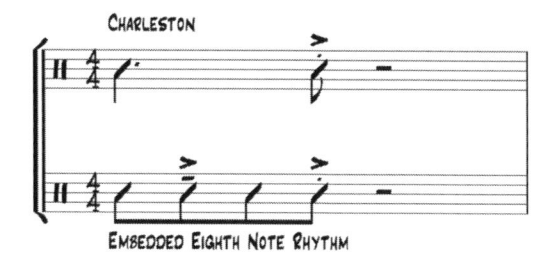

Just as in Chapter 2, when the Shape Method explored how the Charleston Rhythm can be displaced through the measure to create a variety of jazz rhythms, so can the four eighth-notes phrases be shifted to create interesting rhythmic shapes.

The examples below demonstrate how the embedded eighth-notes are progressively delayed by an eighth-note to provide these variations. Please note that in some instances phrases may stop or continue after the ends of these phrase fragments. Note, rhythms that start on beat two or beat three and end right away are rarely used.

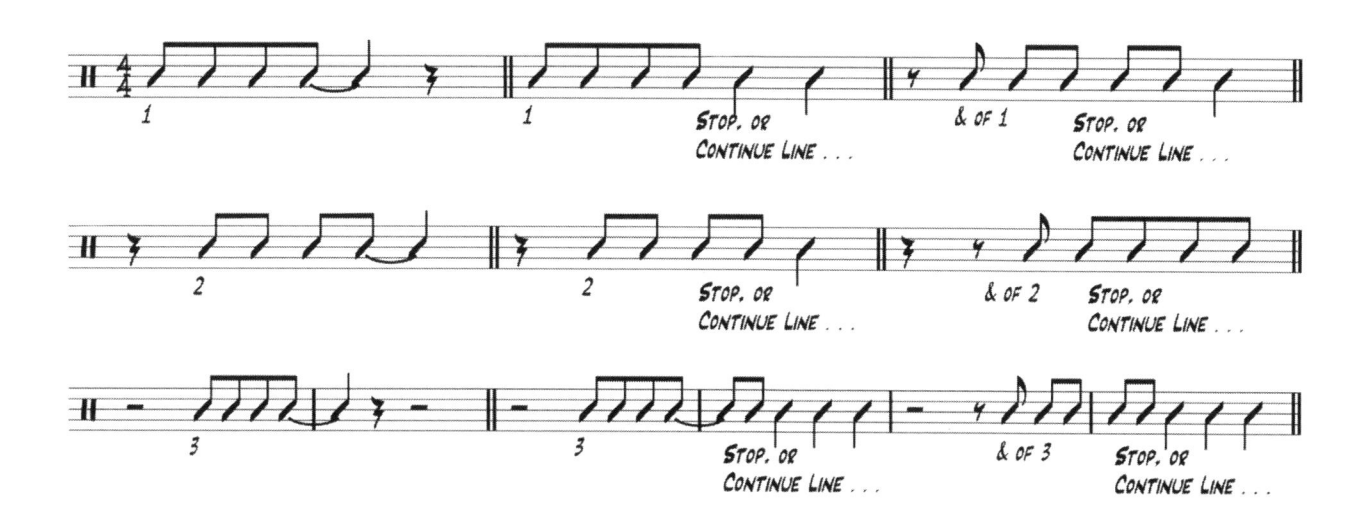

The Shape Method – Chapter 4

The following examples demonstrate these various phrase fragments. The first example starts on beat one (with an anticipation) and ends on the & of 2.

This example also starts on beat one, but continues the phrase.

The third example demonstrates beginning on the & of one and continuing the phrase.

The following example begins on beat two and continues the phrase.

Here is an example of a short phrase, beginning on the & of two and ending on beat four.

The next example demonstrates a common practice of beginning a phrase on beat three and continuing the phrase.

The final example is a phrase that begins on the & of three and continues the phrase.

1st Degree Suspensions

The Shape Method defines **Suspension Tones** as Drive or Gravity resolutions that begin on the beat and resolve off the beat. One way of thinking about Suspensions is to consider them as rhythmically displaced Drive or Gravity Resolution Tones. They will resolve, but they just started in the wrong place – on the beat.

1st Degree Suspension Tones are only one note long and when analyzing are notated with an "S". Here are a few examples of 1st Degree Suspension Tones as they appear when used in solos:

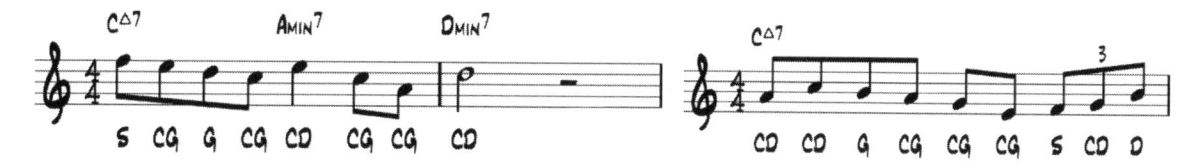

These are the C Major Suspensions moving to their Consonance Tones.

The Shape Method – Chapter 4

These are the C Minor Suspensions moving to their Consonance Tones.

Chapter Summary

- The Charleston Rhythm has an embedded four eighth-note rhythmic shape that can be rhythmically displaced and used as the beginning of melodies.
- 1st Degree Suspensions were defined.

Suggested Listening

Bloomdido

EXERCISES

Composition Exercises

Each of the phrases, except where Suspensions occur, should have Consonance Tones (CT, CD, or CG) on strong beats. Phrase length variance should continue to be observed. Please analyze and label each pitch the with appropriate Shape Method notation.

1) Write a two chorus solo on the following chord changes in which:

    a. Two phrases begin with a 1st Degree Suspension and the appropriate movement to a Consonance Tone

    b. Two phrases begin with a 2nd Degree Chromatic Drive Resolution

    c. Two phrases begin with a 2nd Degree Chromatic Gravity Resolution

    d. One phrase begins with an "& of 1" category rhythm

    e. One phrase begins with an "& of 2" category rhythm

    f. One phrase begins with an "& of 3" category rhythm

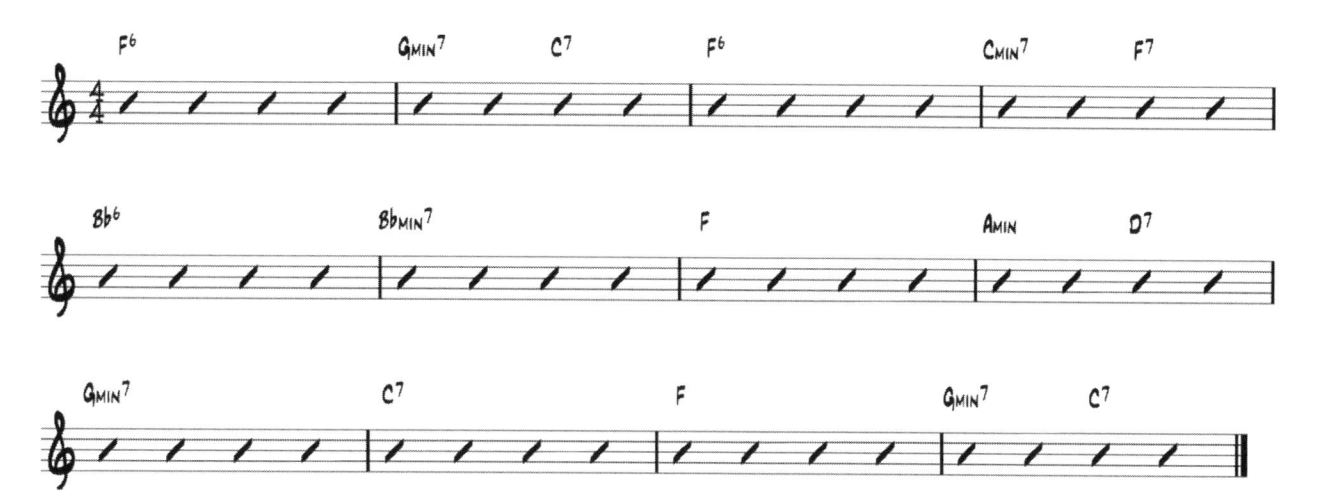

[Musical staff with chord changes:
Line 1: F6 | Gmin7 C7 | F6 | Cmin7 F7
Line 2: Bb6 | Bbmin7 | F | Amin D7
Line 3: Gmin7 | C7 | F | Gmin7 C7]

Performance Exercise

1) Learn and play 1st Degree Suspensions for Major and Minor chords in all keys. (See Etude Supplement, Vol. 1)

Chapter 5 – Motivic Development Through Displacement and Sequence and Interpreting Half-Diminished Chords

Motivic Development

Motivic development is one of the most powerful musical practices that jazz improvisers employ. However, before discussing the development technique of Motivic Development is important to define musical motive. The Shape Method defines a **motive** as a brief musical figure that has specific melodic and rhythmic content. The Charleston rhythm is great place to start discussing motives and motivic development.

In order to qualify as a Shape Method motive and be developed the Charleston rhythm must have some melodic content, and the Shape Method offers a simple and powerful tool to assign melodic content in a harmonic context. Here is the process:

1) Assign Consonance Tone, Resolution Tone, and/or Suspension values to the pitches of a prospective motive.

2) At subsequent recurrences of the motive maintain the same values in the harmony the motive is within.

The example below utilizes the primary Charleston Rhythm and associates it with a melodic shape, creating a motive. The Shape Method analysis of the melodic shape is; the first note is a Suspension, and the second is a Consonance Gravity – "S" and "CG" respectively.

The melodic shape is maintained as the Charleston Rhythm is developed through **rhythmic displacement**, repeating the motive every three beats, as the example below demonstrates. Please note that the "F" on beat four of the first measure is associated with the G7 chord.

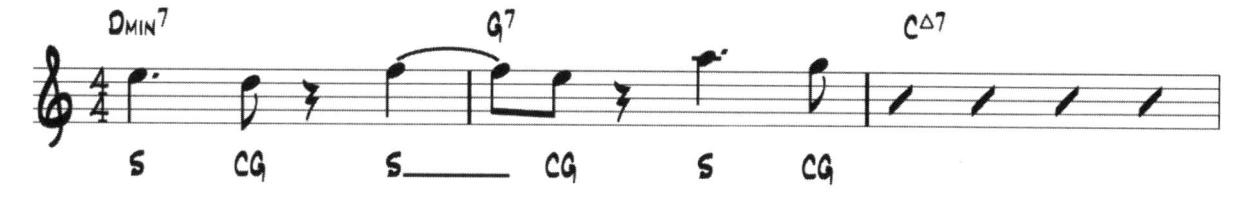

Of course the same procedures can be applied to eighth note rhythms generated from the Charleston Rhythm as discussed in Chapter 4. The example below will use the same procedure, displacing the motive by three beats, but using an eighth note line generated from the Charleston Rhythm as the rhythmic foundation of the motive.

The Shape Method – Chapter 5

[Musical notation: Dmin7 with notes labeled CT CG S CG]

The Shape Method analysis of the melodic shape is; the first note is a Consonance Tone, the second is a Consonance Gravity, third as a Suspension, and fourth as a Consonance Gravity – "CT", "CG", "S", and "CG", respectively.

Motivic development by rhythmic displacement.

[Musical notation: Dmin7 – G7 – C△7 with notes labeled CT CG S CG repeated]

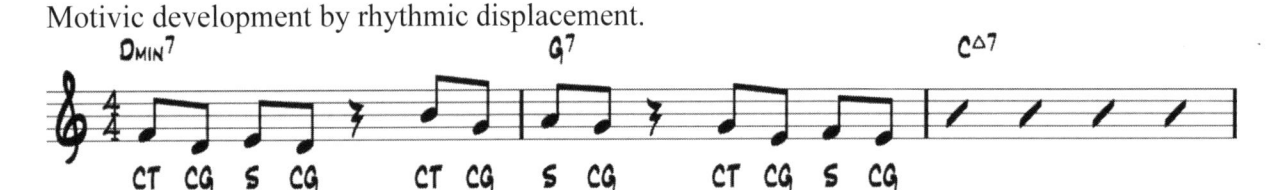

This device presents many opportunities for creating musical form in an improvised setting.

Another powerful tool for Motivic Development is Sequence. The Shape Method defines **sequence** as the direct repetition of a motive at a different pitch level. These transpositions can be real (retaining the absolute interval relationship between the pitches) or tonal (remaining in the same key).

[Musical notation: Real Sequence and Tonal Sequence examples]

Rhythmic displacement can also be applied to sequenced motives to develop interesting phrases.

Half-Diminished Chords

So far the Shape Method has defined many of the common melodic devices used in jazz improvisation; Consonance Tones, Resolution Tones, and Suspensions. Melodic direction has also been a central element in the discussions and definitions. However, these devices have only been applied to 1st Order Major and Minor triads. While focusing on the major and minor triads has laid the foundation for most all jazz chord types, an important type of chord has not been addressed – the Half-Diminished chord.

The Half-Diminished, or Minor Seven-Flat Five, chord has an important function as the ii7 chord in minor keys contexts, and therefore the Shape Method needs a way of working with this important sonority. Fortunately, the path has been blazed by no less than Thelonious Monk. Monk would refer to Half-Diminished chords as "minor 6" chords, and when the contents of the chord are examined, it appears obvious he was right.

[Musical notation: Cmin – Consonance Tones of Cmin – Aø7]

While the chord tones are obviously the same, the Half-Diminished chord has a function of instability that generates harmonic motion, while the min6 chord functions as a stable, though colorful, resting place as the tonic chord of a minor key. However the functional differences do not interfere with how melodies are constructed using the Shape Method because the method focuses on Consonance Tones, where they are located in the measure, and how they are reached – pitch identity, rhythmic location, and melodic direction.

The Shape Method has defined the Consonance Tones of a 1st Order Minor as; 1, min 3, 4, 5, and Maj 6. Further, 1st Order Minor triad Resolutions and Suspensions have been addressed. Therefore, those definitions and practices need only be applied to the Half-Diminished chord built on the 6 of the 1st Order Minor to provide methods of creating melodies on a Half-Diminished chord.

The simple "rule" for Half-Diminished Chords is: apply Shape Method practices to a 1st Order Minor triad, built on the minor 3rd of the Half-Diminished Chord.

Chapter Summary

- Motives were defined as brief musical figures with specific rhythmic and melodic content.

- The technique of Motivic development through rhythmic displacement was discussed.

- The techniques of sequencing motives was discussed.

- Half-Diminished chords were demonstrated to be inversions of Shape Method minor Consonance Tones.

Suggested Listening

Crazeology, One for Daddy 'O

The Shape Method – Chapter 5

EXERCISES

Composition Exercises

Each of the phrases, except where Suspensions occur, should have Consonance Tones (CT, CD, or CG) on strong beats. Phrase length variance should continue to be observed. Please analyze and label each pitch the with appropriate Shape Method notation.

1) Write a two chorus solo on the following chord changes which has:

   a. Two phrases that utilize motivic development through rhythmic displacement

   b. Two phrases that utilize motivic sequencing.

   c. At least three different phrase beginning and three different phrase ending rhythms.

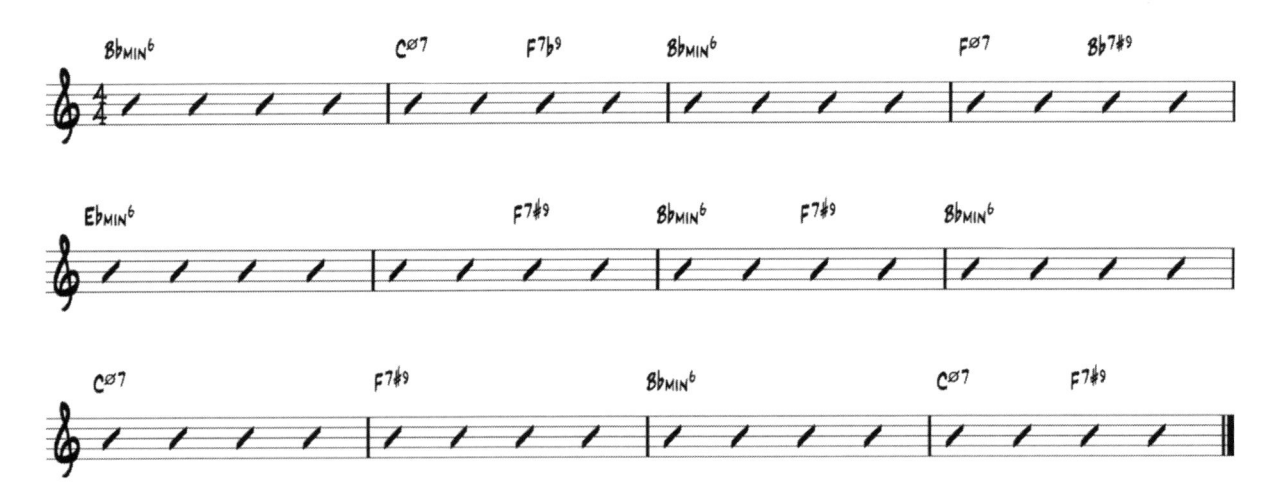

Performance Exercise

1) Learn and play the Resolution Tones of Half-Diminished chords in all keys. (See Etude Supplement, Vol. 1)

Chapter 6 – Using Triplets and Triplet Avoid Rhythms and Bi-Directional Resolutions

Using Triplets

Because jazz rhythm has its foundation in 6/8-like African bell patterns the triplet is the jazz rhythmic division. But, as stated in the Introduction, usually only the first and third triplet division are articulated. The most common exception to this practice is either an ascending or descending arpeggio-like phrase. As seen in the examples below, sometimes the phrase is an arpeggio of the chord and sometimes it is the Consonance Tones of the chord.

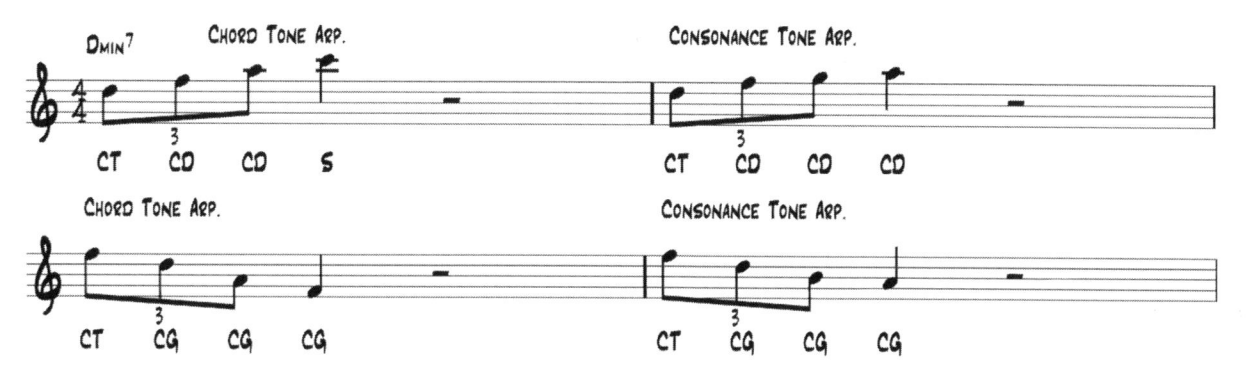

There is rarely more than one beat of triplet arpeggio at a time, and those practices will be addressed in a later chapter.

Though triplets are frequently used on beat two, they can be used on any beat. Below are some examples of triplet use on various beats.

The first example demonstrates a triplet on beat one.

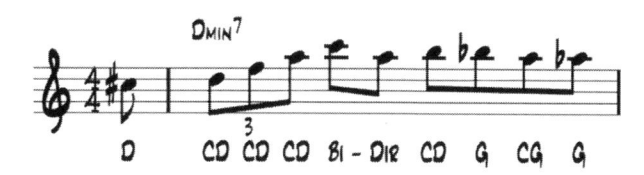

The next example contains a triplet on beat two.

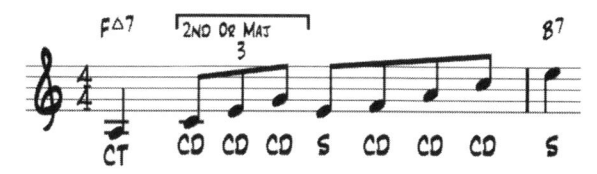

Here is an example of a triplet on beat three.

And the final example on beat four.

Triplet Avoid Rhythms

When using triplets there are certain rhythmic locations that are problematic. Essentially, any triplet rhythm that obscures the location of the pulse is best avoided. The reason these rhythms don't work as well in jazz is that by obscuring the pulse they lessen the strength of the syncopation. Below are examples of what the Shape Method identifies as **Avoid Rhythms**.

Eighth-note triplet Avoid Rhythms

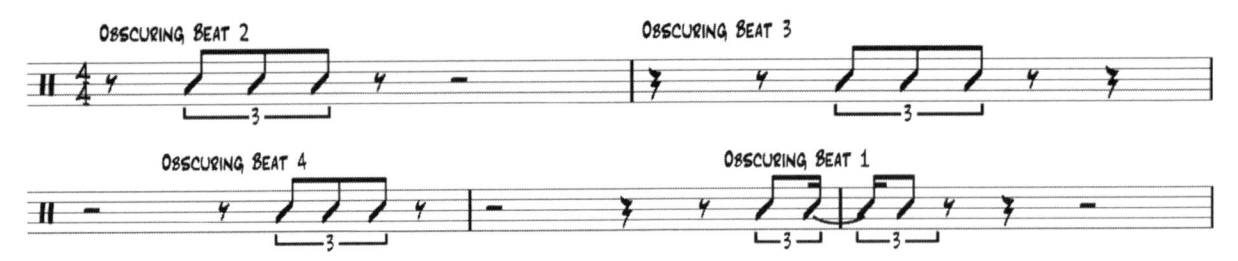

Bi-Directional Resolutions

In Chapter 4 the Shape Method defines a 1st Degree Suspension as a non-Consonance Tone sounding on a beat. This definition means there can be no 2nd Degree Suspensions because, for single-note instruments, there can't be two notes sounding on the same beat. However, there is a very common practice in jazz improvisation where a Suspension is not immediately resolved and the Shape Method defines that as a **Bi-Directional Resolution**. The Shape Method notation is "Bi" on the suspension "-" connecting to "Dir" on the Resolution Tone.

The succinct definition of a Bi-Directional Resolution is; any combination of First Degree Drive and Gravity resolutions, in either order.

These are the C Major and C Minor Bi-Directional Resolutions moving to Consonance Drive and Gravity Tones.

Next are several examples of Bi-Directional Resolutions. The first starts with a Suspension on the major seventh, moves to a Suspension of the second, then has a Gravity Resolution to a Consonance Tone.

This example begins with a Suspension on the augmented fourth, then a Gravity Consonance Tone of the sixth and a Gravity Consonance Tone resolving to the fifth.

Chapter Summary

- Triplets use in arpeggios were discussed.
- Triplet Avoid Rhythms, rhythms that obscure strong beats, were discussed.
- Bi-Directional Resolutions were defined and demonstrated.

Suggested Listening

Quicksilver

EXERCISES

Composition Exercises

Each of the phrases, except where a Suspension or Bi-Directional Resolutions are used, should have Consonance Tones (CT, CD, or CG) on strong beats. Phrase length variance should continue to be observed. Please analyze and label each pitch the with appropriate Shape Method notation.

1) Write a two chorus solo on the following chord changes which has:

    a. One phrase that contains a triplet arpeggio-like phrase starting on beat one.

    b. One phrase that contains a triplet arpeggio-like phrase starting on beat two.

    c. One phrase that contains a triplet arpeggio-like phrase starting on beat three.

    d. One phrase that contains a triplet arpeggio-like phrase starting on beat four.

    e. Six uses of Bi-Directional Resolutions, a minimum of one for each triad Consonance Tone (e.g., 1, 3, min 3, 4, 5, and 6)

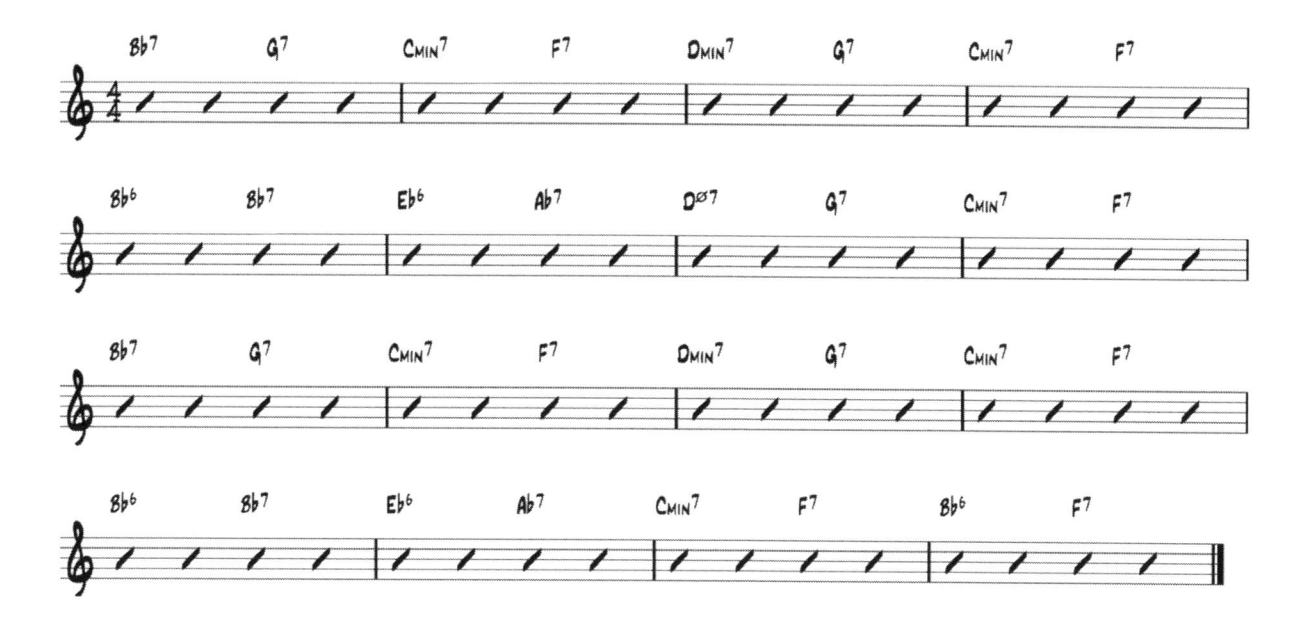

Performance Exercise

1) Learn and play the Bi-Directional Resolutions for Major and Minor chords in all keys. (See Etude Supplement, Vol. 1)

Chapter 7 – Anticipations and 2nd Order Triads and Diminished Chords

Anticipations

The Shape Method defines an **Anticipation** as a note that is articulated before a beat and is associated with the harmonic content of that beat. Anticipations are commonly used in jazz improvisations to provide a sense of "forward motion." By using anticipations improvisers can avoid placing notes on the beat and therefore increase the degree of syncopation and provide a sense of continuance to their lines.

Sometimes anticipations occur at the quarter note pulse, but that usually is reserved for faster tempos when the pulse is more commonly felt in "2." The Shape Method will address that concept in a later chapter. Eighth-note anticipations are more common and the figures below indicate several eighth-note anticipations on each of the beats of a 4/4 meter.

2nd Order Triads

One of the advantages to the Shape Method is that improvisers don't have to deal with the entire chord structure in order to create stylistically appropriate jazz improvisations. Jazz improvisers can create good jazz phrases by applying the principles learned in previous chapters, and the more advanced principles in later chapters, to the foundational Consonance tones of any chord. However, to play in a more complex and complete style improvisers have to not only have more advanced techniques, but be able to use the "upper extensions" of jazz harmonies. The first step in that process is working with the 2nd Order Triads.

As defined in Chapter 1, 1st Order Triads are the root, third (major or minor) and fifth of Major and Minor chords. 2nd Order Triads are built from the fifth of the 1st Order Triad. 2nd Order Triads can be major or minor. Consonance, Resolution, and Suspension Tone devices can be applied to them. Here the Shape Method will discuss two other uses of 2nd Order Triads:

1) Upper Extensions

2) Implications of relative ii chord

The Shape Method – Chapter 7

Upper Extensions

The chart below demonstrates how combining different qualities of major and minor 1st and 2nd Order Triads produce more complete jazz chords.

1st Order Triad	2nd Order Triad	Chord Name
Major	Major	Major 9
Major	Minor	Dominant 9
Minor	Major	Minor, Major 9
Minor	Minor	Minor 9

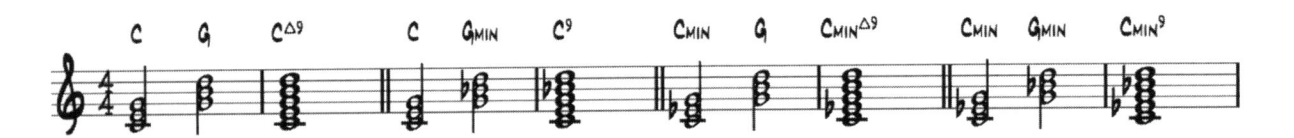

These four chords, along with the Half-Diminished chord already covered in Chapter 5, represent the vast majority of chords used in jazz. More colorful extensions will be discussed in later chapters, but this is a great place to start.

Here are some examples of phrases transcribed from jazz improvisations that utilize the various combinations of 1st and 2nd Order Triads. Note: Shape Method analysis is applied to the 2nd order Triads, not the 1st Order Triads reflected by the chord change.

The first example is a Major/Major (F Maj over Bb Maj) combination.

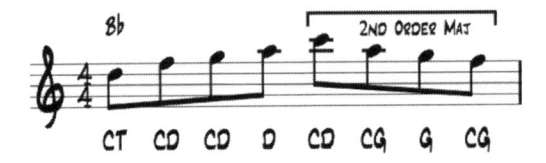

This example is a Minor/Major (Bb Min over Eb Maj) combination.

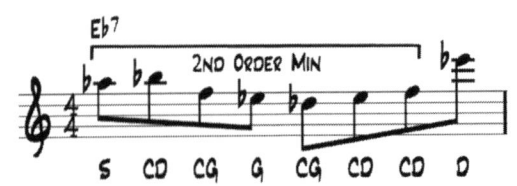

The third example is of a Major/Minor (G Maj over C Min) combination.

And the final example is a Minor/Minor (G Min over C Min) combination.

Implying the Relative ii

Another common use of 2nd Order Triads is to imply the relative ii chord on a V7 chord. Because the chord tones of the ii are the same as the 5, flat 7, and 9 of the Dominant 9 chord jazz improvisers frequently substitute the two changes – playing the ii on the V7 and the V7 on the ii.

For example, the melody transcribed below clearly states the Consonance tones of a G minor Triad on an C Dominant Seven Chord.

Diminished Chords

The final part of the discussion of 2nd Order Triads is how to interpret a Diminished Seven chord. The Shape Method frames discussion of melodic concepts in the context of Major and Minor Triads and since Diminished chords do not contain a Major Third, they must be addressed in the context of combining 1st and 2nd Order Triads.

Diminished chords have three applications:

1) Coloring of a Major Triad.

2) A flexible modulation device because it can function as a Diminished (vii°) chord in four different tonal areas.

3) A Dominant, Flat Nine chord without the root.

The Shape Method already addresses the first instance through the use of Suspensions. The second application, while important, is not relevant to the discussions of melodic and rhythmic shape discussed here. Therefore, the Shape Method concentrates on the third application when discussing Diminished chords.

Diminished Chords should be treated as 1st Order Major and 2nd Order Minor (with flat five) WITHOUT the root. The Consonance Tones of a Diminished Seventh Chord are 3, 5, b7, b9 and Resolutions should be applied as they are to other chords. The basic procedure is:

1) Go DOWN a Major Third from the root of the Diminished Chord

2) Build a 1st Order Major and 2nd Order Minor (flat five) Triad combination.

3) Construct melodies using the 3, 5, 7, & b9 of that chord as Consonances Tones.

The example below, while not flatting the fifth on the 2nd Order Minor Triad, is good example of this practice.

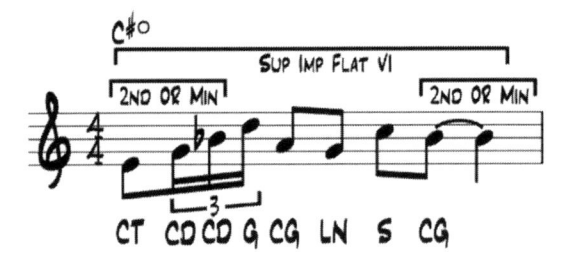

Chapter Summary

- Anticipations were discussed.
- 2nd Order Triads were defined and discussed.
- Diminished Seventh Chords were discussed.

Suggested Listening

Eternal Triangle, Blues for Alice

The Shape Method – Chapter 7

EXERCISES

Composition Exercises

Each of the phrases, except where Suspensions or Bi-Directional Resolutions occur, should have Consonance Tones (CT, CD, or CG) on strong beats. Phrase length variance should continue to be observed. Please analyze and label each pitch the with appropriate Shape Method notation.

1) Write a two chorus solo on the following chord changes which has:

   a. Two phrases each that utilize eighth-note anticipation of beat 1 and beat 3.

   b. Two phrases that utilize 2nd Order Triads as Upper Extensions

   c. Two phrases that utilize 2nd Order Triads to imply the relative ii chord on a V7.

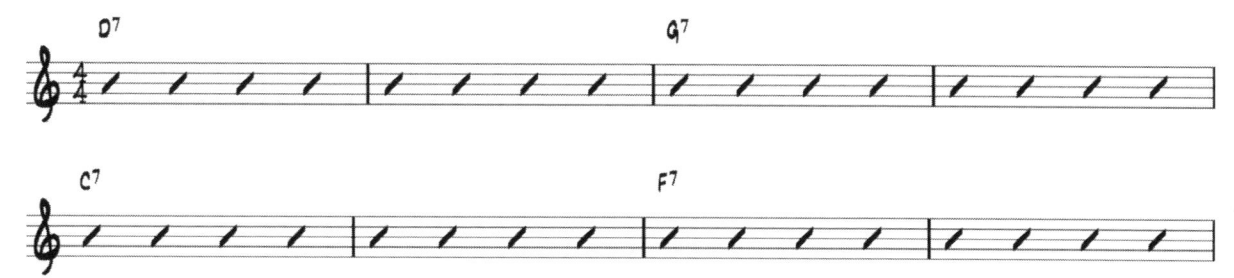

[Musical staff with chord changes: D7 | G7 | C7 | F7]

2) Write a one chorus solo on the following chord changes in which the phrases have two each that utilize eighth-note anticipation of beat 1 and beat 3.

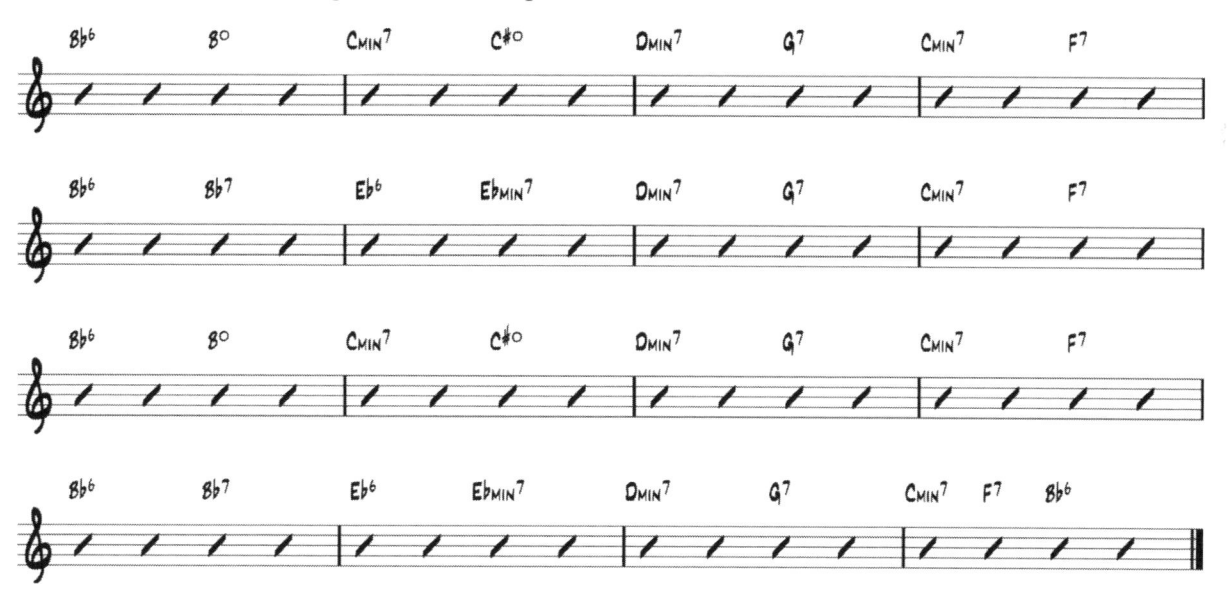

[Musical staff with chord changes:
Bb6 B° Cmin7 C#° | Dmin7 G7 Cmin7 F7
Bb6 Bb7 Eb6 Ebmin7 | Dmin7 G7 Cmin7 F7
Bb6 B° Cmin7 C#° | Dmin7 G7 Cmin7 F7
Bb6 Bb7 Eb6 Ebmin7 | Dmin7 G7 Cmin7 F7 Bb6]

Performance Exercise

1) Learn and play the all four combinations of 1st and 2nd Order Triads in all keys. (See Etude Supplement, Vol. 1)

Chapter 8 – Varying Rhythmic Values and Anchor Phrases

Varying Rhythmic Values

While the eighth note is the most common rhythmic value in jazz improvisation it is not the only one. In fact, varying the rhythmic values in an improvisation is one of the easiest and most effective ways to add interest to a solo.

A simple way to vary rhythm values is to alternate quarters and eighths.

Combining triplets with eighths notes is also a common practice

And, of course, combining variations of the Charleston Rhythm with quarter, eighth, and triplet notes results in lines with rhythmic interest.

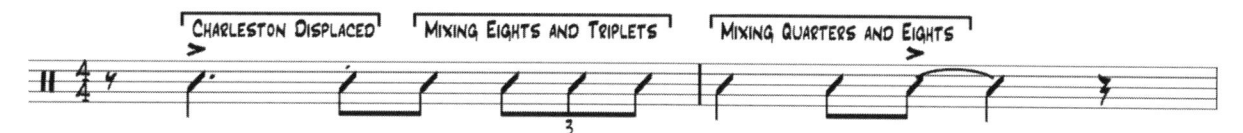

Anchor Phrases

The Shape Method defines an **Anchor Phrase** as a phrase in which one or more notes are repeated while a third note experiences First Degree Drive or Gravity Resolutions. Anchor Phrases are common in jazz improvisations and have several components.

The components of Anchor Phrases are:

1) Resolution Types
    a. Drive
    b. Gravity
2) Resolution Color
    a. Diatonic
    b. Chromatic
3) Suspensions
    a. 1st Degree
    b. Bi-Directional Resolutions
4) Harmonic Rhythm
    a. Fast or Slow
    b. Long or Short

Based on the number of qualities that can be combined in different ways, it is easy to see how Anchor Phrases provide a vast resource for jazz improvisation.

The example below is a common model of an Anchor Phrase that contains Gravity Resolutions (note the chromatic passing of the D to the B with the "anchoring" A).

The next example is a rhythmic variation on the phrase.

And another variation, this one changing the harmonic rhythm and extending the phrase over several measures.

The next example is a common model of an Anchor Phrase using Drive Resolutions (note the chromatic passing of the A to the B).

Here is a variation using anticipations.

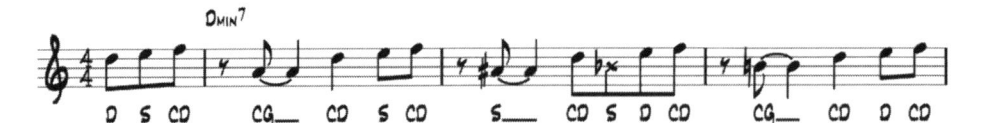

And a second variation that speeds the harmonic rhythm.

The following Anchor Phrases contain diatonic Bi-Directional Resolutions.

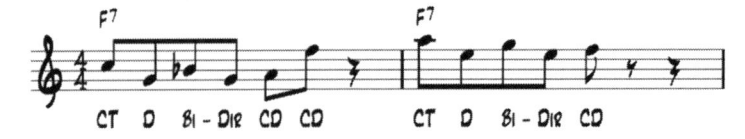

And these contain chromatic Bi-Directional Resolutions.

Chapter Summary

- Phrases can generate interest by varying their rhythmic content.
- Anchor Phrases were defined and discussed.

Suggested Listening

Groovin' High, Half Nelson

The Shape Method - Chapter 8

EXERCISES

Composition Exercises

Each of the phrases, except where Suspensions or Bi-Directional Resolutions occur, should have Consonance Tones (CT, CD, or CG) on strong beats. Phrase length variance should continue to be observed. Please analyze and label each pitch the with appropriate Shape Method notation.

1) Write a four chorus solo on the following chord changes which has:

   a. One phrase each combining:

      i. Alternating Eighths and Quarters

      ii. Mixing Triplets with Eighths

      iii. Mixing a Charleston Variation with Eights

      iv. Mixing a Charleston Variation with Triplets

   b. Two phrases that utilize Gravity Anchor Phrases (Write on the changes that have slower harmonic rhythm)

   c. Two phrases that utilize Drive Anchor Phrases (Write on the changes that have slower harmonic rhythm)

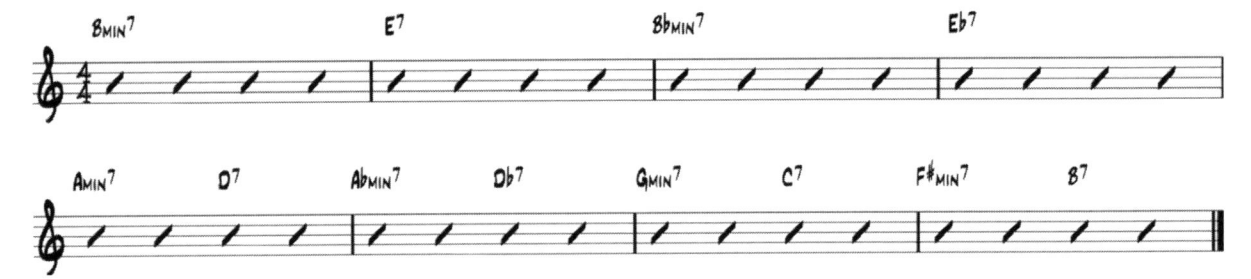

[Musical staff with chord changes: Bmin7, E7, Bbmin7, Eb7, Amin7, D7, Abmin7, Db7, Gmin7, C7, F#min7, B7]

Performance Exercise

1) Learn and play the example Anchor Phrases in all keys, then create your own and learn and play. (See Etude Supplement, Vol. 2)

Chapter 9 – Multiple Pickup Notes and Introduction to Direction Changing

Multiple Pickup Notes

In previous chapters the Shape Method has only addressed eighth-note lines derived from the Charleston Rhythm and therefore has limited the number of notes to four. Jazz improvisers need to be able to use greater number of consecutive eighth-notes when appropriate.

The following are rhythmic examples of multiple pickup notes to beat one.

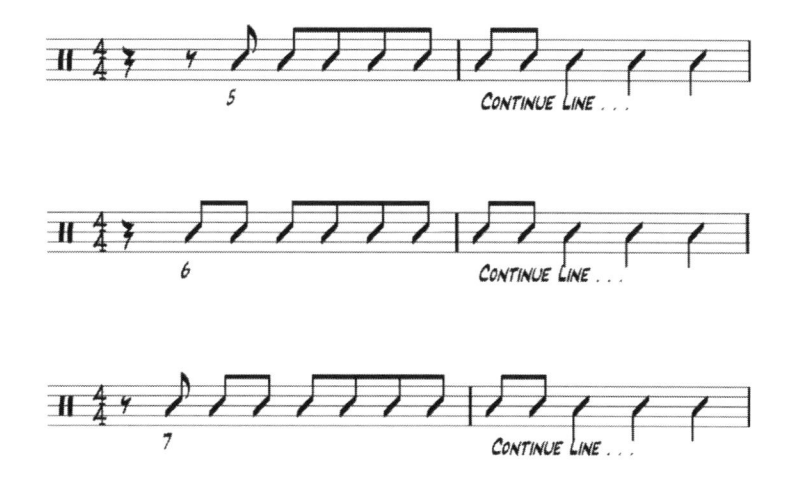

By utilizing different length of pickup notes the jazz improviser can add interest to their phrases.

The first example is of a five-note pickup phrase.

This example demonstrates a six-note pickup phrase

The final example is of a seven-note pickup phrase.

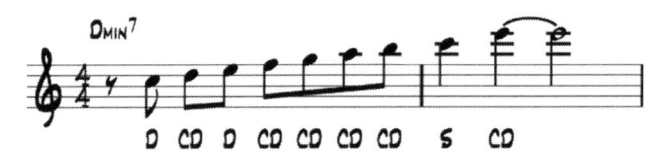

Direction Changing

One of the essential features of jazz improvisation is the angularity of the melodies. Jazz improvisers accomplish rhythmic angularity, as the Shape Method discussed in Chapter 8, by varying the rhythmic values within the phrase. The phrases of jazz improvisation are also made angular through changing melodic direction. This chapter begins to address the various methods employed to accomplish those changes. But first, a little more information about the practice of direction changing.

Direction Change Analysis

The Shape Method has analyzed several solos by master jazz musicians for phrase features. The solos are Miles Davis - *Solar*, Hank Mobley – *All The Things You Are*, Johnny Griffin – *Blues Up And Down*, Bud Powell – *Bouncin' With Bud*, Clifford Brown – *Split Kick*, Dexter Gordon – *Cheesecake*, Woody Shaw – *There Will Never Be Another You*, Dizzy Gillespie – *Sometimes I'm Happy*, Charlie Parker – *Groovin' High*, and John Coltrane – *Freight Train*. These musicians and solos were chosen because of their important contributions to the jazz language. These analysis reveal some interesting information about Shape in jazz solos.

The first analysis concerns how phrases begin. The chart below demonstrates the great variety regarding these musicians' choices of which direction to begin the phrase – ascending or descending. The chart is arranged by the percentage of Descending Phrases. It is interesting to note the similarities between players who were associated with each other during the early parts of their careers: Gillespie/Coltrane, Davis/Parker, and Gordon/Shaw.

Musician	Phrases Begins Descending	Phrase Begins Ascending
Gillespie	25%	75%
Coltrane	26.67%	73.33%
Mobley	33.33%	66.67%
Powell	36.36%	63.64%
Davis	37.50%	62.50%
Parker	39.13%	60.87%
Brown	48.57%	51.43%
Griffin	50%	50%
Gordon	63.16%	36.84%
Shaw	71.43%	28.57%

The Shape Method – Chapter 9

This chart demonstrates the average phrase length in measures. Notice again, the great differences in phrase lengths between these master improvisers. This not only demonstrates the variety of phrase length, but also hints at some of the underpinnings of individual style. For example, a frequent comment about Miles Davis' phrasing is "he uses a lot of space." Upon further examining his phrase structures the Shape Method demonstrates that he's not leaving a lot of space between phrases, he's leaving <u>frequent space</u> between phrases – two completely different things.

Musician	Average Phrase Length in Measures
Davis	2
Coltrane	2.18
Griffin	2.54
Gillespie	2.75
Parker	2.91
Gordon	2.94
Powell	3
Shaw	3.19
Brown	3.68
Mobley	4

The following chart addresses the average number of direction changes per phrase. Because of the various techniques employed to change direction, sometimes it is difficult to judge if it is a true direction change or not. The best effort was made to be consistent, but there may be some variations in interpretation.

Musician	Average Number of Direction Changes Per Phrase
Davis	2
Griffin	2.67
Brown	3
Gillespie	3
Gordon	3.15
Shaw	3.19
Coltrane	3.22
Parker	3.67
Mobley	4.11
Powell	4.9

The preceding chart also demonstrates the ubiquity of direction change in master improvisers' solos. The Shape Method will now address several techniques used to change direction in solos, starting with ornamentation.

The simplest method of ornamentation used in jazz solos is the Upper and Lower Neighbor Tone. The Shape Method defines **Neighbor Tones** as pitches that occur off the beat, after a note sounds on the beat, and resolves back to the original note. Upper Neighbor Tones are indicated by "UN" and Lower by "LN."

The following example demonstrates one of the primary uses of ornamentation, to provide the feeling of motion to a phrase that is actually not moving. Below is the original phrase.

There is no motion at all during the first beat-and-a-half of the measure. While this is an acceptable jazz rhythm, improvisers sometimes choose to give this phrase forward motion by ornamenting the first note with an Upper Neighbor.

In the following example, Lower Neighbor Tones are used to extend the motion of the melody.

This type of ornamentation is sometimes used as a device to change direction of the melody. In the example below the melody changes direction when the Upper Neighbor E Flat resolves to the D. (Also note, that this line uses the 2nd Order Minor triad, G min)

In the following example a Lower Neighbor Tone (F#) is used to change the direction of the melody.

Chapter Summary

- Multiple pickup notes were discussed.

- Direction Changes in solos were analyzed.

- Neighbor Tones were defined and demonstrated to be a way to extend melodic activity and a Direction Change technique.

Suggested Listening

Prince Albert, Bluesette

The Shape Method – Chapter 9

EXERCISES

Composition Exercises

Each of the phrases, except where Suspensions or Bi-Directional Resolutions occur, should have Consonance Tones (CT, CD, or CG) on strong beats. Phrase length variance should continue to be observed. Please analyze and label each pitch the with appropriate Shape Method notation.

1) Write a four chorus solo on the following chord changes which has:

   a. One phrase that uses five pickup notes to beat one

   b. One phrase that use six pickup notes to beat one

   c. One phrase that use seven pickup notes to beat one

   d. Two phrases that utilize Upper Neighbor Tones to extend melodic motion

   e. Two phrases that utilize Lower Neighbor Tones to extend melodic motion

   f. Two phrases that utilize Upper Neighbor Tones to change the direction of the melody

   g. Two phrases that utilize Lower Neighbor Tones to change the direction of the melody

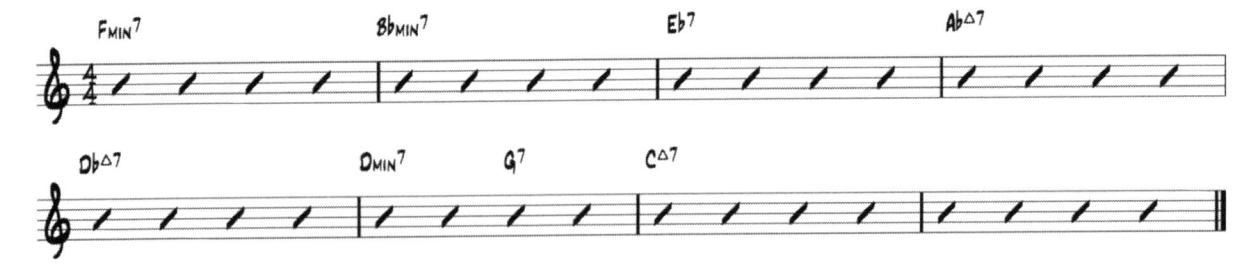

Performance Exercise

1) Learn and play Upper and Lower Neighbor Tone ornaments to 1st Order Major and Minor Triads in all keys. (See Etude Supplement, Vol. 2)

Chapter 10 – Multiple Syncopations and Direction Change via Arpeggio/Scale Phrases

Multiple Syncopations

Syncopation, accenting notes in normally unaccented rhythmic locations, is a hallmark of jazz improvisation. Sometimes syncopations can be strung together to create even stronger forward motion in the melody. A common practice is to put together two quarter-note length notes off the beat. The examples below demonstrate the examples of two consecutive quarter note-length syncopations.

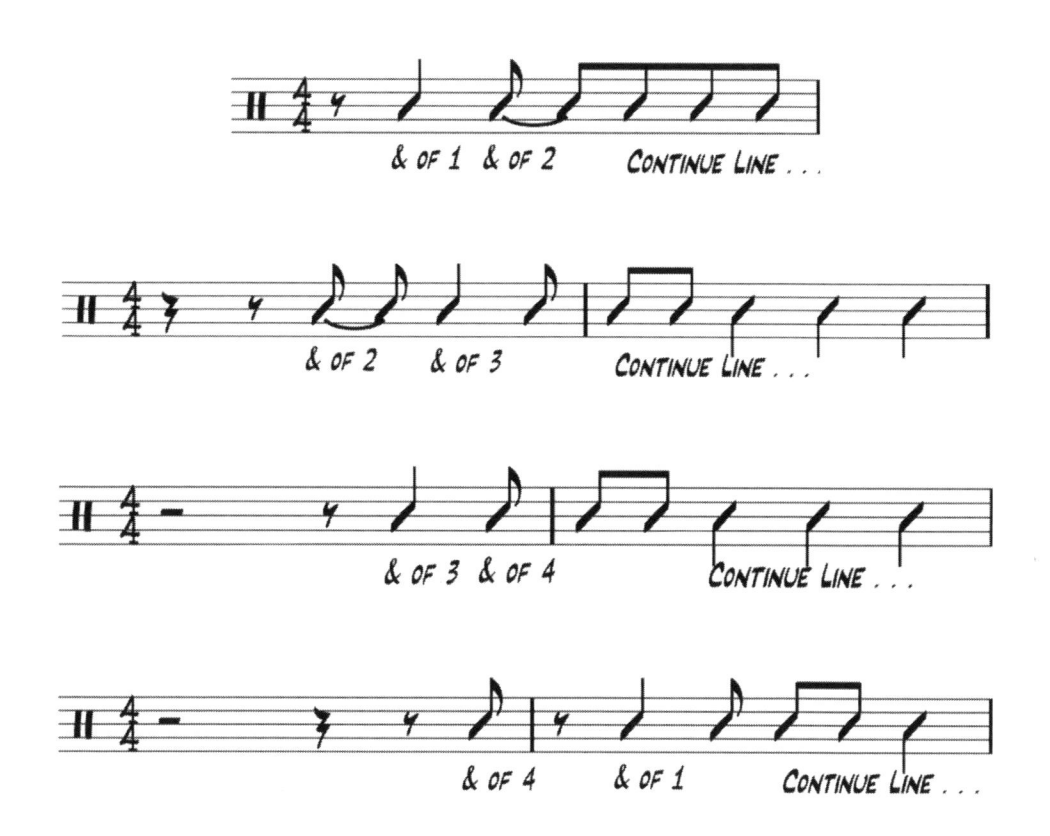

Arpeggio/Scale Alternations

Direction change within jazz phrases is one of the most ubiquitous characteristics of jazz improvisations. Direction change can be accomplished through a number of techniques, and in Chapter 9 the Shape Method discussed ornamentation as a direction change device. This chapter will explore alternating Arpeggio and Scalar passages as direction change techniques.

The Shape Method – Chapter 10

Jazz improvisers frequently change direction of their melodies by alternating arpeggio and scalar figures. These alternations can be of various combinations:

1) Ascending to Descending

   a. Arpeggio then Scale

   b. Scale then Arpeggio

2) Descending to Ascending

   a. Scale then Arpeggio

   b. Arpeggio then Scale

The following figures demonstrate how direction change can be accomplished by alternative arpeggio and scalar figures.

The first example is an Ascending Arpeggio and Descending Scalar phrase.

The next is an Ascending Scalar and Descending Arpeggio phrase.

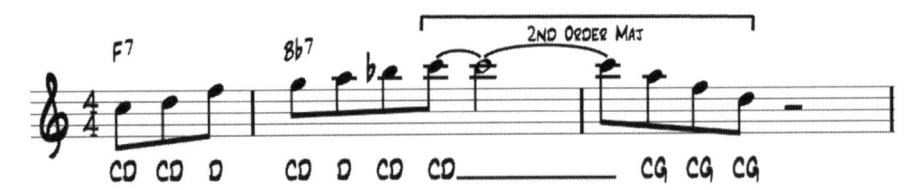

This example demonstrates a Descending Scalar and Ascending Arpeggio phrase.

The final example shows a Descending Arpeggio and Ascending Scalar phrase.

Chapter Summary

- Multiple syncopations were discussed.
- The practice of changing direction through alternating Scalar and Arpeggiated melodic materials was discussed and demonstrated.

Suggested Listening

Donna Lee, Joy Spring

The Shape Method – Chapter 10

EXERCISES

Composition Exercises

Each of the phrases, except where Suspensions or Bi-Directional Resolutions occur, should have Consonance Tones (CT, CD, or CG) on strong beats. Phrase length variance should continue to be observed. Please analyze and label each pitch the with appropriate Shape Method notation.

1) Write a two chorus solo on the following chord changes which the has:

   a. One phrase that changes direction by alternating an ascending arpeggio with a descending scalar phrase

   b. One phrase that changes direction by alternating a ascending scalar with a descending arpeggio phrase

   c. One phrase that changes direction by alternating a descending arpeggio with an ascending scalar phrase

   d. One phrase that changes direction by alternating a descending scalar with an ascending arpeggio phrase

   e. One phrase each that begins with multiple syncopations starting on:

      i. & of 1

      ii. & of 2

      iii. & of 3

      iv. & of 4

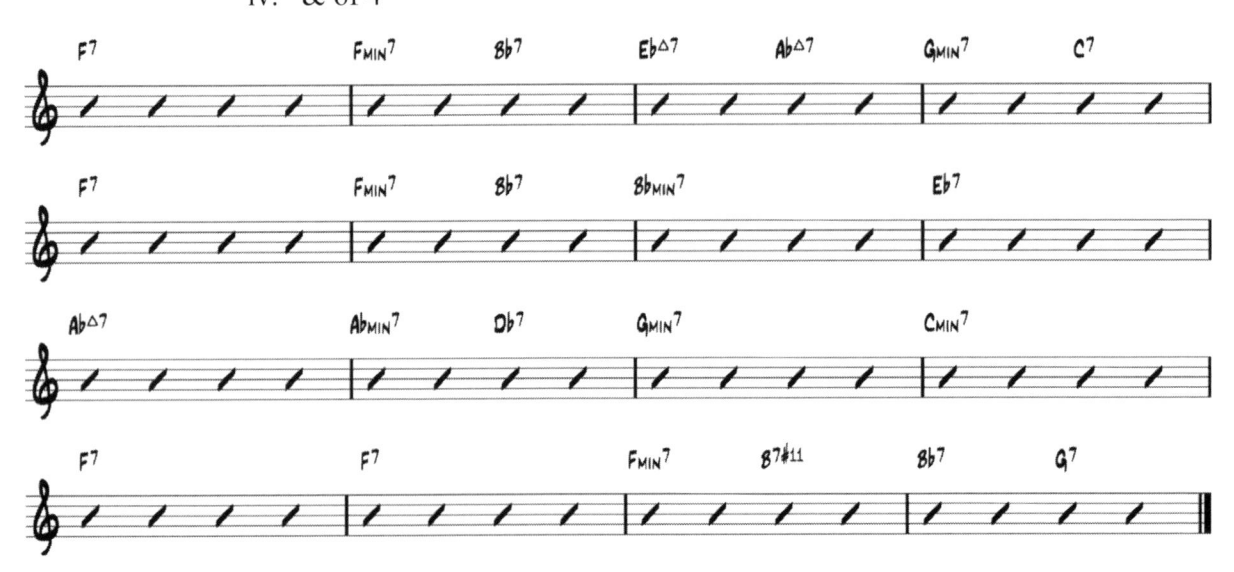

[Chord changes:
Line 1: F7 | Fmin7 Bb7 | Eb△7 Ab△7 | Gmin7 C7
Line 2: F7 | Fmin7 Bb7 | BbMin7 | Eb7
Line 3: Ab△7 | AbMin7 Db7 | Gmin7 | Cmin7
Line 4: F7 | F7 | Fmin7 B7#11 | Bb7 G7]

Performance Exercise

1) Learn and play the all four combinations of 1st and 2nd Order Triads in all keys. (See Etude Supplement, Vol. 2)

Chapter 11 – Micro-Resolutions with Triplets and Direction Change via Octave Displacement

Micro-Resolutions with Triplets

The Shape Method defines Micro-Resolutions as resolutions that move faster than eighth-notes. The first Micro-Resolution practice discussed is the triplet.

In Chapter 6 the common use of triplet was discussed and it was noted that in most cases triplets are used for only one beat at a time – with an exception. That exception is the triplet in Micro-Resolution.

Triplet Micro-Resolutions are commonly used to connect Consonance Tones a minor third apart through chromaticism. The following examples demonstrate common usage.

These are examples of "one way" connections, and they can be Drive Resolutions -

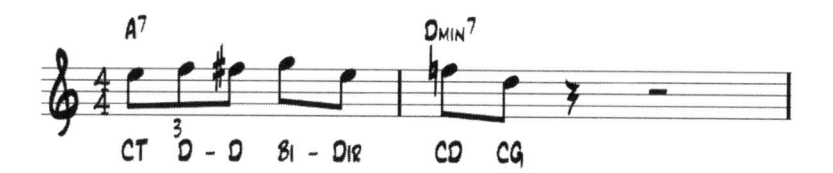

or Gravity Resolutions.

Frequently Triplet Micro-Resolutions return to the original Consonance Tone – thereby creating consecutive beats of triplets. The Shape Method defines these phrases as **Returning Triplet Micro-Resolutions**. The following example indicates the use of Returning Triplet Micro-Resolutions, a combination of Drive and Gravity Resolutions.

Sometimes, whole-steps and half-steps are mixed to connect Consonance Tones a Major Third apart.

Direction Change through Octave Displacement

A simple way to create direction change in a jazz improvisation is **Octave Displacement**. Octave Displacement is defined by the Shape Method as moving a note of a melody to a different octave. This can be done at the Resolution Tone or the Consonance Tone.

The first example demonstrates Octave Displacement at the Resolution Tone.

The Shape Method analyses the G on the & of four as a Gravity Resolution Tone that has experienced Octave Displacement.

This example demonstrates Octave Displacement at the Consonance Tone.

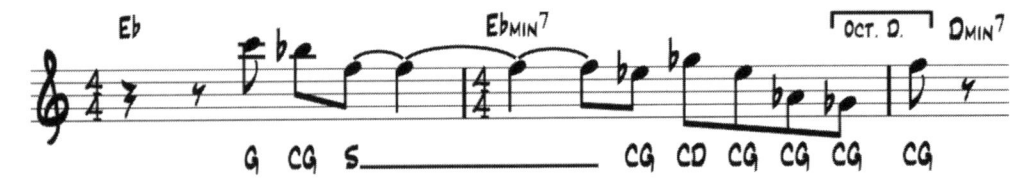

The Shape Method analyses the final F as a Gravity Consonance Tone that has experienced Octave Displacement.

Chapter Summary

- Micro-Resolutions were defined and Micro-Resolutions using Triplets were demonstrated.

- Octave Displacement as a technique for Direction Change was discussed and demonstrated.

Suggested Listening

Little Willie Leaps and Mayreh

The Shape Method – Chapter 11

EXERCISES

Composition Exercises

Each of the phrases, except where Suspensions or Bi-Directional Resolutions occur, should have Consonance Tones (CT, CD, or CG) on strong beats. Phrase length variance should continue to be observed. Please analyze and label each pitch with appropriate Shape Method notation.

Write a two chorus solo on the following chord changes which has:

1) One phrase that uses <u>Drive</u> Triplet Micro-Resolutions of Minor Third.

2) One phrase that uses <u>Gravity</u> Triplet Micro-Resolutions of Minor Third.

3) One phrase that uses <u>Drive</u> Triplet Micro-Resolutions of Major Third.

4) One phrase that uses <u>Gravity</u> Triplet Micro-Resolutions of Major Third.

5) One phrase that uses <u>Drive/Gravity</u> Triplet Micro-Resolutions of Minor Third.

6) Two phrases that change direction by using Octave Displacement of the Resolution Tone.

7) Two phrases that change direction by using Octave Displacement of the Consonance Tone.

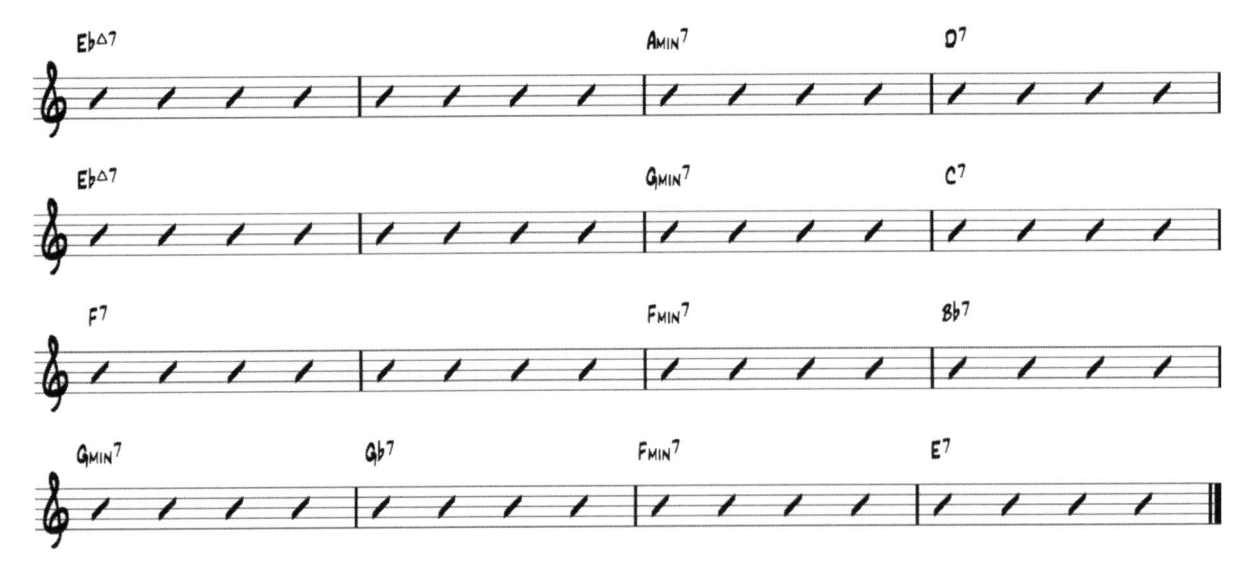

Eb△7		Amin7	D7
Eb△7		Gmin7	C7
F7		Fmin7	Bb7
Gmin7	Gb7	Fmin7	E7

Performance Exercise

1) Learn and play Drive, Gravity, and Drive/Gravity chromatic Triplet Micro-Resolutions between all minor thirds. (See Etude Supplement, Vol. 2)

Chapter 12 – Adjusting Harmonic Rhythm for Slow Tempos and Direction Change via Suspension Escape Tones

Adjusting Harmonic Rhythm for Slow Tempos

When improvising at slow tempos it is important to maintain a sense of forward motion. The common method for maintaining forward motion is to sub-divide the pulse into even eighth-notes. This allows the improviser to conceptualize the rhythms of their melodies in sophisticated ways while still maintaining the original feel of the ballad.

The example below is a notated version of this conceptualization.

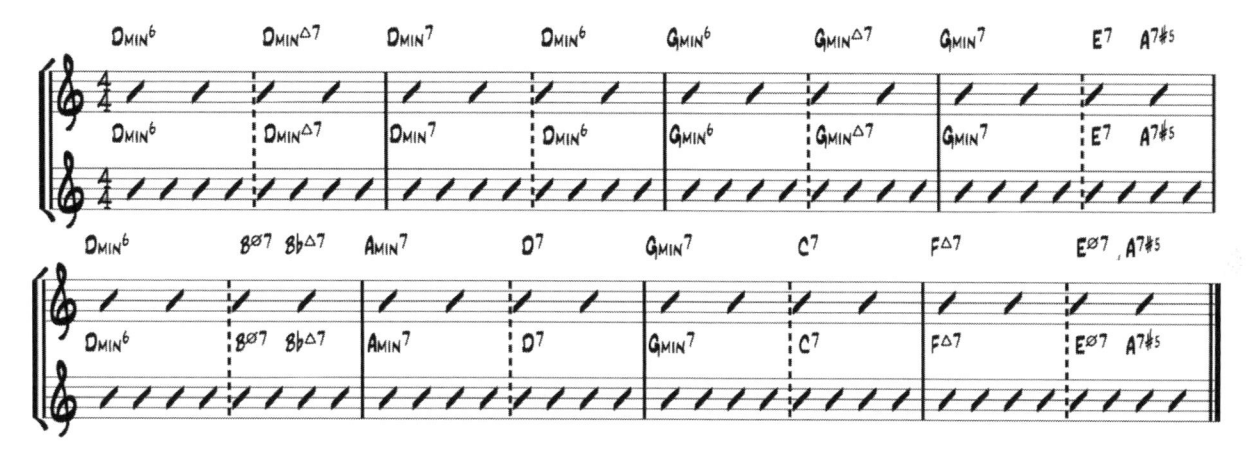

The dotted barline mid-measure indicates the double-time feel of the lower staff chord changes. This practice is the reason that jazz ballads are "straight eighth" ballads, so the players can imply this double-time feel.

However, it is important to understand that the triplet is still the basis for jazz rhythm and the triplet feel must be maintained in these slow tempo settings. To accomplish this, the triplet division is applied to the pulse structure of the lower line.

The example below indicates the pulse and subdivision structures of the first measure. The upper system is the original tempo and harmonic rhythm, the lower system is the <u>implied</u> swing feel upon which the improvisers can work and the comping instruments can play. Please note, this implied swing feel doesn't mean that the drums and bass should play at the faster division, they should "stay home" with the original pulse, allowing the solo and comping instruments the flexibility of working with the triplet structure.

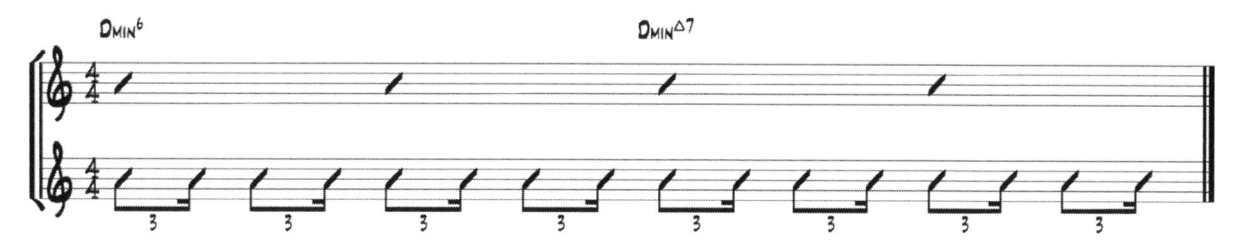

Direction Change through Suspension Escape Tones

The Shape Method defines **Suspension Escape Tones** as beginning with a suspension then moving to any note OTHER than the complimentary Bi-Directional Resolution. Suspension Escape Tones come in two varieties; Upper Escape ("UE") and Lower Escape ("LE"). The following examples start with a Bi-Directional Resolution and change a note to create a Suspension Escape Tone.

The first of the following examples has a Bi-Directional Resolution on beat four (F# to E) resolving to a Drive Consonance Tone (F).

This example of a Suspension Escape Tone has the same line except the E on the & of four has been changed to a G#, creating an Upper Escape Tone.

The first of this set of examples has a Bi-Directional Resolution on beat two (A to F#) resolving to a Drive Consosnance Tone (G).

This example of a Suspension Escape Tone has the same line except the G on beat 3 has been changed to a B, creating a Lower Suspension Escape Tone on the F#.

Chapter Summary

- At extremely slow tempos, the harmonic rhythm should be felt at double-time tempo and swung at that pulse rate.

- Suspension Escape Tones were defined and demonstrated.

Suggested Listening

A Night In Tunisia and Tempus Fugue-It

The Shape Method – Chapter 12

EXERCISES

Composition Exercises

Each of the phrases, except where Suspensions or Bi-Directional Resolutions occur, should have Consonance Tones (CT, CD, or CG) on strong beats. Phrase length should still vary in length. Please analyze and label each pitch the with appropriate Shape Method notation.

Write a two chorus solo on the following chord changes which has:

1) The first chorus in the original time feel.

2) The second chorus in the double-time feel. (Leave the meter the same and write sixteenth level divisions.)

3) Two phrases that change direction using Upper Suspension Escape Tone.

4) Two phrases that change direction using Lower Suspension Escape Tone.

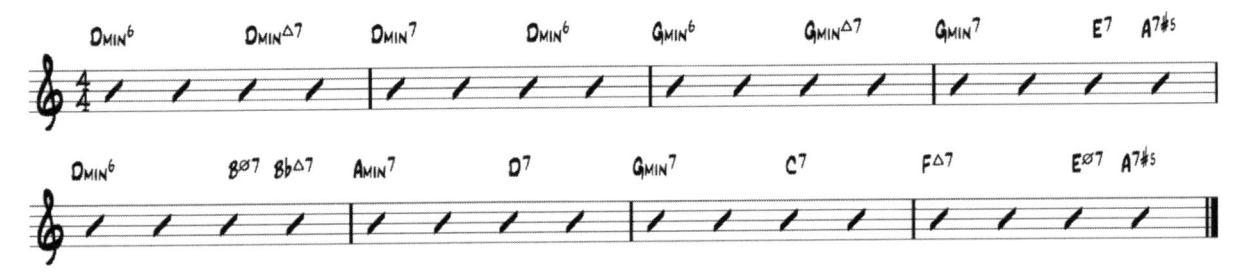

[Chord chart: Dmin6 | Dmin△7 | Dmin7 | Dmin6 | Gmin6 | Gmin△7 | Gmin7 | E7 A7#5 | Dmin6 | B⌀7 Bb△7 | Amin7 | D7 | Gmin7 | C7 | F△7 | E⌀7 A7#5]

Performance Exercise

1) Compose, learn, and play several Suspension Escape Tone Resolutions.

Chapter 13 – Adjusting Harmonic Rhythm for Fast Tempos and Direction Change via Consonance Escape Tones

Adjusting Harmonic Rhythm for Fast Tempos

Louis Armstrong essentially taught musicians how to swing, and one of the most important lessons was how to apply flexible pulse concepts within an improvised solo. Or stated another way, how to spontaneously contract and expand the pulse within the phrase.

In Chapter 12 the Shape Method discusses techniques for adding forward motion to tunes in slow tempos by doubling the pulse rate. This chapter discusses ways to apply the converse concept to tunes in fast tempos.

When the tempo of a song gets fast, say above 240 beat per minute, it opens up a whole new level of rhythmic sophistication to the improviser by allowing them to phrase in half-time.

The example below demonstrates this half-time conception.

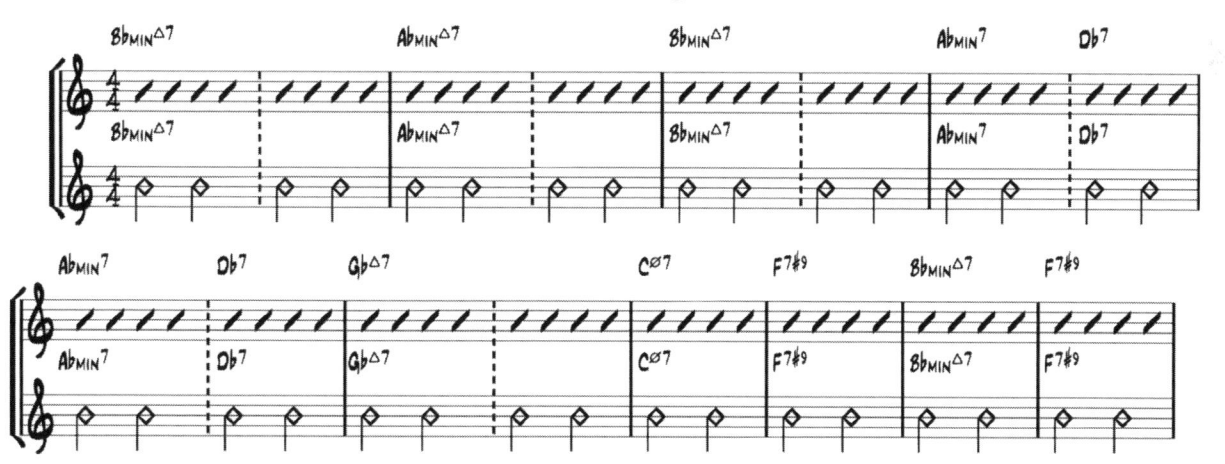

The upper system indicates the original, rapid tempo. The lower system indicates the half-time pulse speed at which improvisers can choose to play when tempos reach faster speeds.

As in Chapter 12, the example below indicates the pulse and subdivision structures of the first two chord changes. The upper system is the original tempo and harmonic rhythm, the lower system is the <u>implied</u> half-time feel upon which the improvisers can work and the comping instruments can play. Please note, this implied swing feel doesn't mean that the drums and bass should play at the slower division, they should "stay home" with the original pulse, allowing the solo and comping instruments the flexibility of working with the half-time structure.

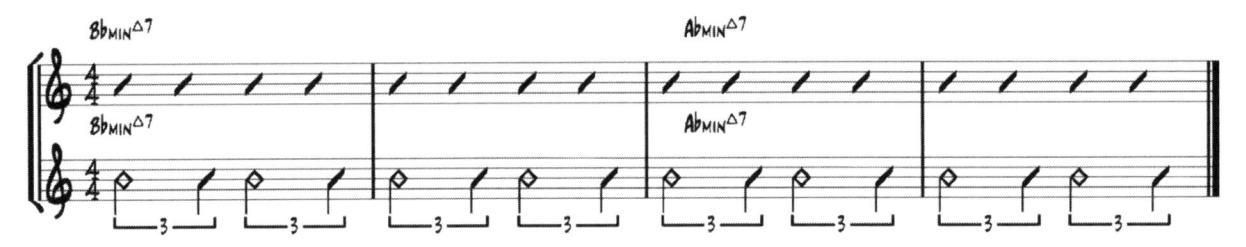

Consonance Escape Tones

The Shape Method defines **Consonance Escape Tones** as Consonance Tones that skip between strong beats, almost always down, missing one or more intervening Consonance Tones. The most common use of a Consonance Escape Tone is to delay the arrival at a Consonance Tone on a strong beat. The example below demonstrates this practice.

If the melody had continued down to the next consonance tone of the chord a Consonance Tone of A would have sounded on strong beat three. By using a Consonance Escape Tone of E, the line can change direction, keep moving and finally reach the Consonance Tone on one of the next measure. This example also demonstrates the almost exclusive usage of Consonance Escape Tones, moving from the third of the chord down to the fifth. Here's a more colorful example of the same type of usage.

Chapter Summary

- At extremely rapid tempos, the harmonic rhythm should be felt at a slower pulse and swung at that pulse division.

- Consonance Escape Tones were defined and demonstrated.

Suggested Listening

Nica's Dream and The Night Has A Thousand Eyes

The Shape Method – Chapter 13

EXERCISES

Composition Exercises

Each of the phrases, except where Suspensions or Bi-Directional Resolutions occur, should have Consonance Tones (CT, CD, or CG) on strong beats. Phrase length variance should continue to be observed. Please analyze and label each pitch the with appropriate Shape Method notation.

1) Write a two chorus solo on the following chord changes which has:

   a. The first chorus at the original pulse speed.

   b. The second chorus at the half-time pulse speed. (Leave the meter the same and write quarter-note triplet divisions.)

   c. At least four usages of Consonance Escape Tones to change direction of the melody.

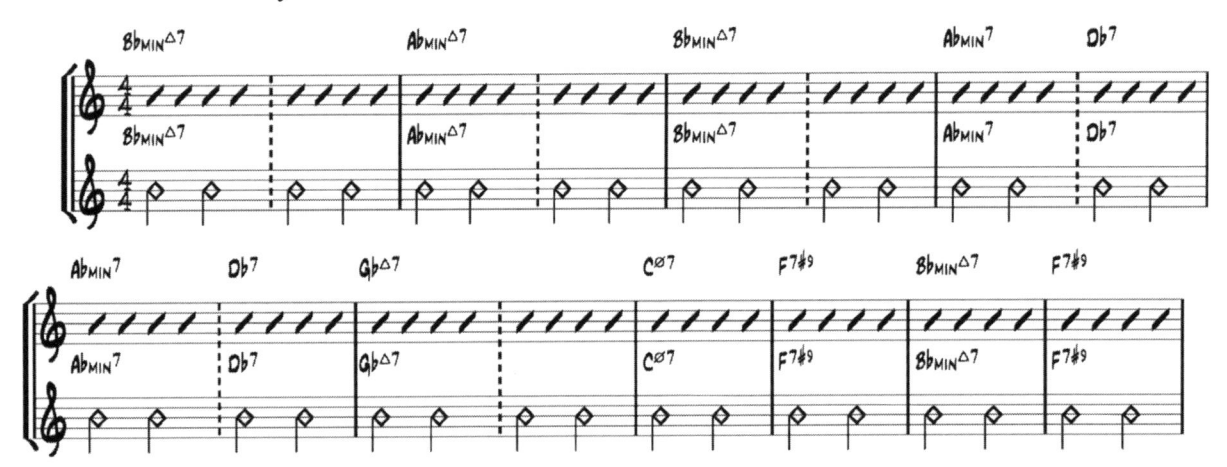

Performance Exercise

1) Learn and play Consonance Escape Tones in all Major and Minor Triads in all keys.

Chapter 14 – Micro-Resolutions with Sixteenths and Extended Bi-Directional Resolutions

Micro-Resolutions with Sixteenths

In Chapter 11 the Shape Method discussed Triplet Micro-Resolutions, here Micro-Resolutions with Sixteenths are the focus.

As with Triplet Micro-Resolutions, Sixteenth Micro-Resolutions are frequently used to connect Consonance Tones a third apart using chromaticism. However, these Consonance Tones are Major thirds apart instead of Minor.

The example below demonstrates a typical usage.

Another common use of Sixteenth Micro-Resolutions is in the construction of double-time phrases. An important consideration in double-time phrases is the doubling of the harmonic rhythm that is implied by the speed of the notes. This means that strong beats are no longer only beats one and three, but occur on every beat of 4/4 meter. The result is that Consonance Tones, or judicious use of Suspensions are called for on every beat of the measure.

In addition to arpeggios of Consonance Tones, two phrases are commonly used in constructing double-time melodies; Returning Sixteenth Micro-Resolutions and Extended Bi-Directional Resolutions.

The Shape Method defines Sixteenth Returning Micro-Resolutions as phrases that begin on a Consonance Tone, move away through 2nd Degree Drive or Gravity Resolutions, and then return to the initial Consonance Tone.

Here are two examples, the first Gravity Resolutions, the second Drive Resolutions.

Extended Bi-Directional Resolutions

In Chapter 6 the Shape Method introduced the concept of Bi-Directional Resolutions and defined them as any combination of First Degree Drive and Gravity resolutions, in either order. These are common shapes in jazz improvisations, but there are more complex structures based on the same principle – those are called Extended Bi-Directional Resolutions.

Extended Bi-Directional Resolutions ("E-Bi-Dir" in Shape Method notation) are defined as a three note resolution that begins with a Drive or Gravity Resolution off the beat, jumps to the complimentary side of the Consonance Tone and resolves back with two more notes (usually half-steps) in the complimentary direction. The initial pitch of an E-Bi-Dir is usually a Gravity Resolution.

Extended Bi-Directional Resolutions are most commonly used when the harmony is static for a measure or more. They are very effective methods of providing motion when the harmony is slow or at rest.

The first example demonstrates a common use of an E-Bi-Dir. The "F" on the & of 1 is the first Suspension Tone above the target "E", then the line moves to "D", the complimentary note of the Bi-Dir Resolution, but is then <u>extended</u> through the chromaticism of the "D#" until the Drive Consonance Tone of the "E" is finally reached on beat three.

The following example is more complex, beginning with a Suspension Tone, and including two E-Bi-Dir in one measure.

The final example also demonstrates added complexity through the use of E-Bi-Dir Resolution, the 2nd Order Triad, and a Suspension Lower Escape Tone.

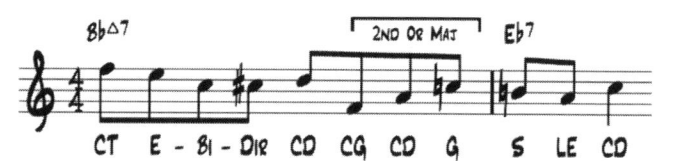

These examples demonstrate the use of consecutive Extended Bi-Directional Resolutions at the Sixteenth Micro-Resolution.

Chapter Summary

- Micro-Resolutions using Sixteenth notes were defined and demonstrated.
- Extended Bi-Directional Resolutions were defined and demonstrated.

Suggested Listening

Fingers, Hot House

The Shape Method – Chapter 14

EXERCISES

Composition Exercises

Each of the phrases, except where a Suspension or Bi-Directional Resolutions are used, should have Consonance Tones (CT, CD, or CG) on strong beats. Phrase length variance should continue to be observed. Please analyze and label each pitch the with appropriate Shape Method notation.

1) Write a two chorus solo on the following chord changes which has:

   a. Four phrases that utilize sixteenth-note Micro-Resolutions to connect major third intervals.

   b. Four phrases that utilize Extended Bi-Directional Resolutions.

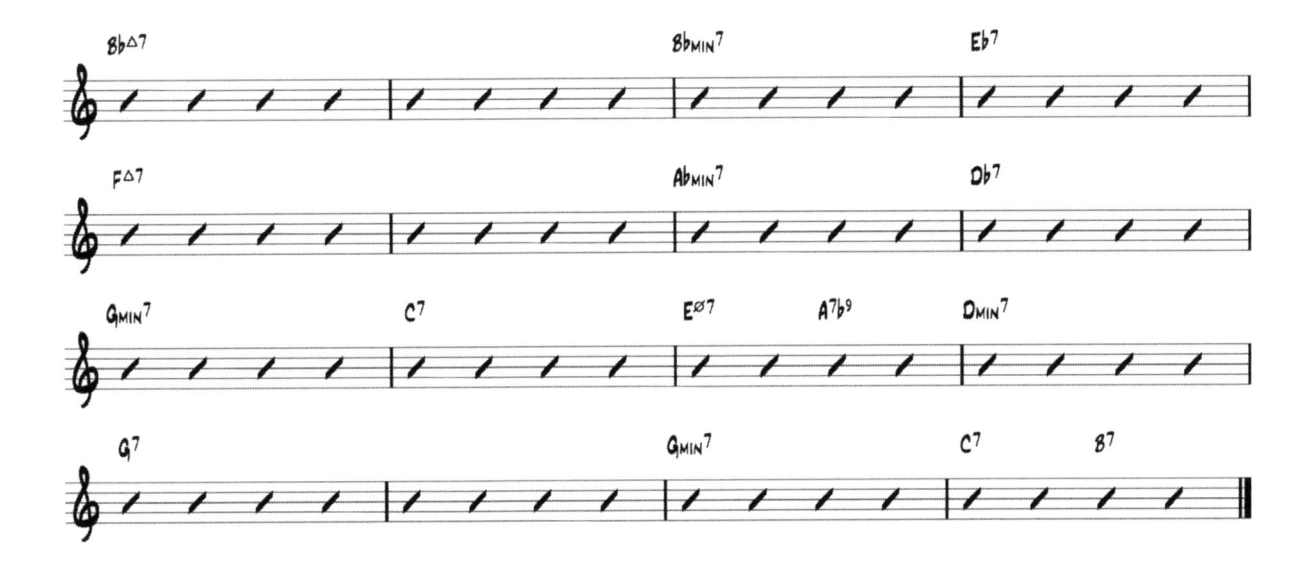

Bb△7		Bbmin7	Eb7
F△7		Abmin7	Db7
Gmin7	C7	Eø7 A7b9	Dmin7
G7		Gmin7	C7 B7

Performance Exercise

1) Learn and play the Extended Bi-Directional Resolutions for Major and Minor chords in all keys. (See Etude Supplement, Vol. 2)

Chapter 15 – Re-Barring and Harmonic Rhythm Anticipation and Delay

Re-Barring

Bebop melodies and improvisations frequently have rhythmically angular melodies. The rhythmic structures can be thought of as the temporary over-laying of different meters on the Common Time pulse. The Shape Method refers to this practice as **Re-barring**. Both of the examples below are in 4/4 time, but the rhythms of the melody are analyzed in mixed meters when appropriate. When the meters implied by the melodies are not in 4/4, the numbers below the staff reflect the beats in 4/4 and the chord changes above are associated with the original 4/4 meter.

The first example is a 12-bar blues. The eight beats of measures one and two are Re-barred into two measures of 3/4 and one of 2/4. This practice is repeated in measures five and six of 4/4 time.

To get a feeling for this complex rhythmic structuring try this exercise:

1) Tap your foot on 2 and 4 of 4/4 time

2) Sing the rhythm of the melody

3) Conduct the meters indicated

The second example is based on the A section of Rhythm Changes and is much more complex.

The first five measure of 4/4 time (20 beats) are divided into six measures: Two of 3/4, two of 4/4, and two more of 3/4 before finally resolving the rhythmic dissonance on bar six of the original changes, the E Flat harmony.

The final three measures (12 beats) immediately create more rhythmic tension through re-barring. The first ending divides the beats into four measures: One of 2/4, two of 4/4, and one of 2/4 – a palindromic beat structure. The second ending is more repetitive and provides for a stronger rhythmic cadence by dividing the beats into four measure: One of 2/4, one of 4/4, one of 2/4 and the final measure of 4/4.

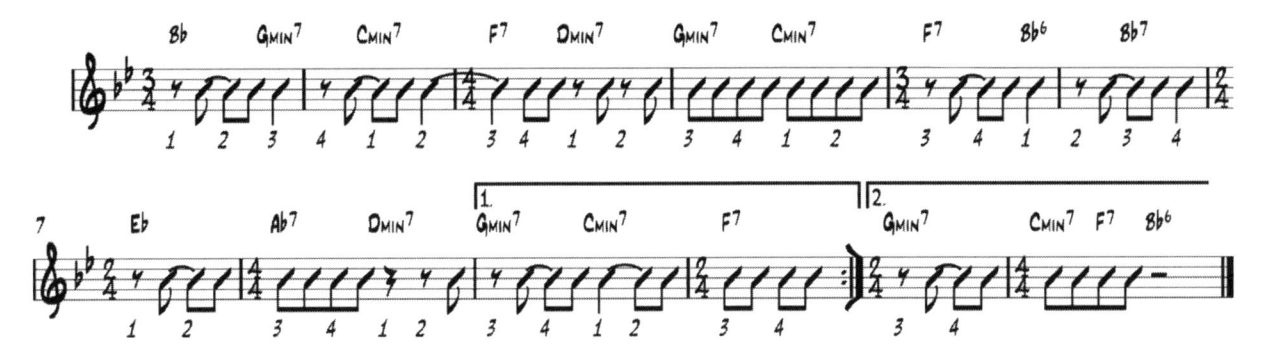

Try the tap/sing/conduct exercise to experience the rhythmic complexity of this melody.

Harmonic Rhythm - Anticipation

The Shape Method defines **Harmonic Rhythm** as the speed, measured in number of pulses, at which the harmonies change. To play a melody that indicates the new harmonic area by at least two beats (in 4/4 meter) is the definition of Harmonic Anticipation ("Har Antic" in Shape Method notation).

Max Roach once told a story about playing with a new bass player in the Charlie Parker Quintet. Charlie Parker was a master at Harmonic Anticipation, so much so that players inexperienced with working with him would frequently jump ahead in the chord changes. They did this because the melodies that Parker played were so strongly in the next harmony that the bass players would think they had made a mistake and would try to correct it. Max said when Parker would start one of those phrases he'd turn to the bass player and yell, "Stay with me!" to keep the harmonic rhythm straight and let Parker's melodies work against the harmonies the way they were intended.

A common Harmonic Anticipation is to play a phrase from the upcoming harmonic resolution on the last two beats of the Dominant. If these melodies avoid the root of the resolution chord they contain no unwanted suspensions and reinforce the resolution.

Another very common use of Harmonic Anticipation is to draw notes from the next chord change so the melody has forward motion to that resolution. Note: As in 2nd Order Triads, the Shape Method analysis refers to the Anticipated or Delayed harmonic area.

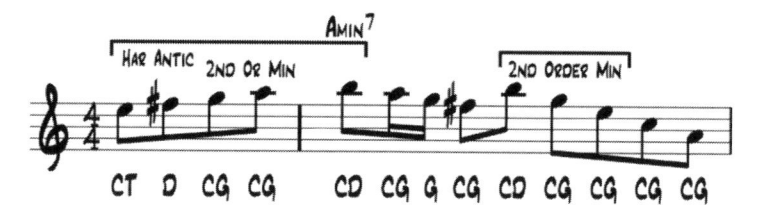

Harmonic Anticipation can also be used to "elide" a ii chord in a ii-V harmonic context by playing figures on the V chord while the ii is sounding as in the example below.

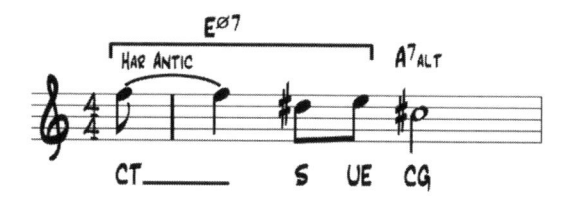

Sometimes, as in the following example, Harmonic Anticipations are strung together.

Harmonic Rhythm – Delay

Just as "Har Antic" is the anticipation of the preceding harmony by at least two beats, Harmonic Delay, "Har Delay" is the delay of the arrival at the new harmonic by at least two beats.

Harmonic Delay is most commonly used when the melody the improviser needs to reach a logical conclusion.

Here is an example of a lengthy Harmonic Delay. The first chord is Gmin6 and the melody is played from that change for the next two measures as the chords change to D7#9 and Fmin6

Both these examples of Harmonic Delay demonstrate a common characteristic, the strong beats of the harmony are frequently Consonance Tones of the delayed harmonic area (A, Bb (#5), and D are CTs of D7, and C and D are CTs of Fmin).

Chapter Summary

- Re-barring was defined and examples were analyzed.
- Phrases using Harmonic Anticipation were discussed and demonstrated.
- Phrases using Harmonic Delay were discussed and demonstrated.

Suggested Listening

Have You Met Miss Jones, But Not for Me, Just Friends

The Shape Method – Chapter 15

EXERCISES

Composition Exercises

Each of the phrases, except where a Suspension or Bi-Directional Resolutions are used, should have Consonance Tones (CT, CD, or CG) on strong beats. Phrase length variance should continue to be observed. Please analyze and label each pitch the with appropriate Shape Method notation.

1) Write a two chorus solo on the following chord changes in which:

    a. Two phrases utilize Harmonic Anticipation.

    b. Two phrases utilize Harmonic Delay.

2) Write a one chorus solo on the following chord changes that use Re-barring to create complex metric and rhythmic structures. Make sure to use <u>distinctive</u> rhythmic gestures when implying meters other than 4/4.

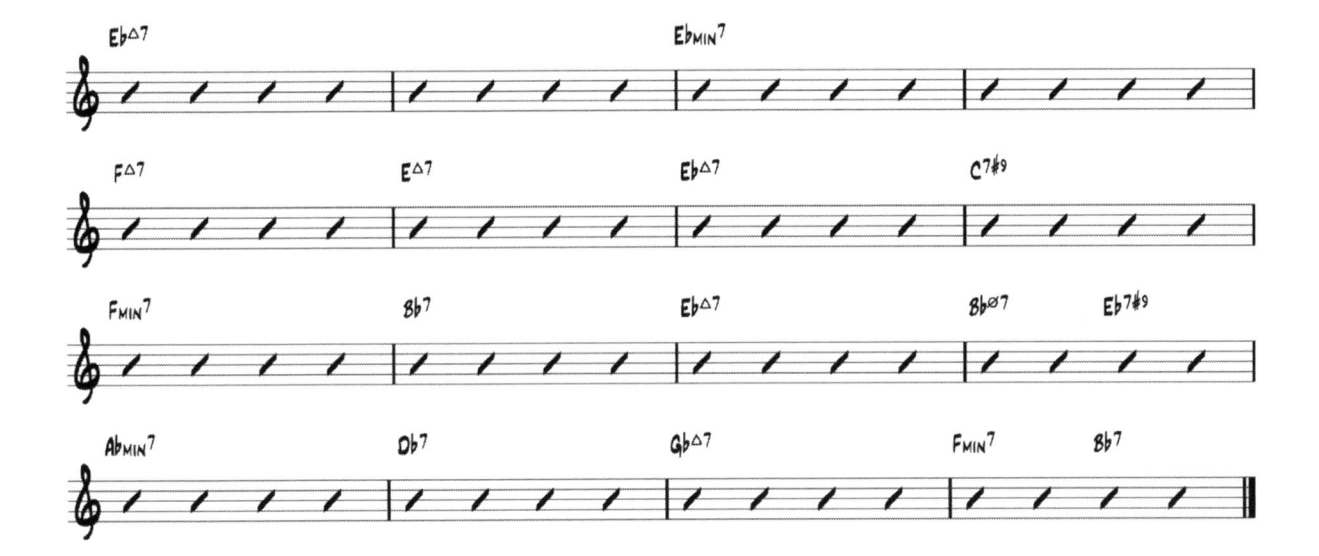

Eb△7		Ebmin7	
F△7	E△7	Eb△7	C7#9
Fmin7	Bb7	Eb△7	Bbø7 ... Eb7#9
Abmin7	Db7	Gb△7	Fmin7 ... Bb7

Performance Exercise

1) Play various scales placing accents on notes to demonstrate Re-barring. For example, create a re-barring structure of 3/4, 3/4, 2/4 and accent the downbeat of each measure.

Chapter 16 – The Son and Rumba Clave and Super-Imposition on Minor and Major Triads

The Son and Rumba Clave

The Shape Method has discussed the Clave several times and drawn much rhythmic information from the history of the Clave. The emphasis has been on the "3-Side" of the Clave (the rhythm of a dotted-quarter on one and an eighth-note on the & of 2) from which the Charleston Rhythm is drawn. The next two chapters will discuss contemporary Claves, "Son" and "Rumba."

In Chapter 1 the Shape Method discussed the evolution of the 6/8 Clave from an African Bell Pattern.

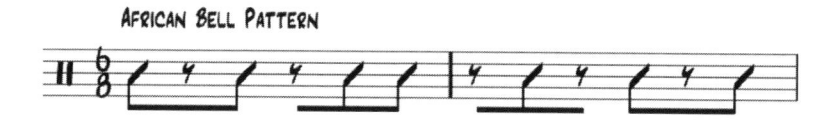

The articulations at the ends of the measures were removed resulting in a Clave rhythm.

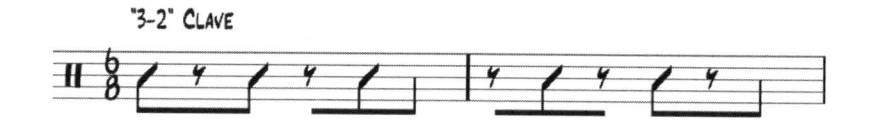

In contemporary use the pattern is frequently "straightened out," with even eighth-notes, and placed in a 4/4 meter. This example demonstrates a 4/4 meter, "3-2" Son Clave pattern.

The pattern can be reversed, placing the two-accent measure of the pattern first. This is a more common practice in contemporary latin jazz.

One of the most important decisions to make when playing latin jazz is which "side" should start the pattern. The information needed to make this decision is in the rhythm of the melody – the accent on the & of two needs to occur when the melody has an articulation on the & of two. This is the most crucial determinant because the Clave and melody need to support each other.

Another common, but not universal, condition is when the melody has an articulation on beat one, the Clave should be oriented to the "2-Side." Conversely, when there is no melody articulation on beat one the Clave should start with the "3-Side."

The reason this usually works is because of rhythmic balance in most melodies. The Clave is a two measure phrase, with rhythmic "stasis" and less activity on the "2-Side" and more activity and syncopation on the "3-Side." Melodies also follow this pattern of greater "stasis" in one measure (frequently a note sounding on the first beat), and greater syncopation in the second measure. By examining the beginning of melodic phrases and the accent patterns the correct orientation of the Clave can be determined.

The Rumba Clave is very similar to the Son, the difference being on the "3-Side" of the pattern. In the Rumba Clave the third accent in the "3-Side" is delayed by a half-beat, occurring on the & of 4. Here is an example of a "3-2 Rumba Clave."

And here, the Clave is turned to demonstrate a "2-3 Rumba Clave."

The same procedures apply for Rumba Clave to determine how to orient the Clave to the melody; the Clave must support the syncopations in the melody, and the balance of "stasis" to syncopation must be maintained.

Balance Between Harmonic and Rhythmic Activity

The Shape Method identifies the need for a balance between the amount of harmonic activity and rhythmic activity. When one of the elements becomes very active the other needs to defer to retain the correct balance. A balance between the number of chord changes in a measure and the number of syncopations of the melody needs to be maintained.

Super-Imposition on Minor Triads

The Shape Method defines Super-Imposition as melodies that employ a triad other than 2nd or 3rd Order Triads. The Method will begin by exploring Super-Impositions ("Sup Imp") on Minor chords.

When discussing Super-Impositions, it is necessary to understand that, in almost all cases, Consonance Tones of the foundational chord are present, but only triad tones of the super-imposition. The table below lists the consonant super-impositions on a minor triad.

Minor Triad	Super-Imposition	Combined Tones	Resultant Chord
C minor	B Flat Major (bVII)	C, D, Eb, F, G, A, Bb	C minor 9
C minor	E Flat Major (bIII)	C, Eb, F, G, A, Bb	C minor 13

This example demonstrates the most common "Sup Imp" on a minor chord, a Major Triad based on the minor third of the chord. This "Sup Imp" has so many common Consonance Tones that it is barely discernable as a "Sup Imp," only the Flat 7 of the minor seven chord revealss the super imposition.

The next example demonstrates a variation on the same shape that uses the "Sup Imp" of the Flat VII Major.

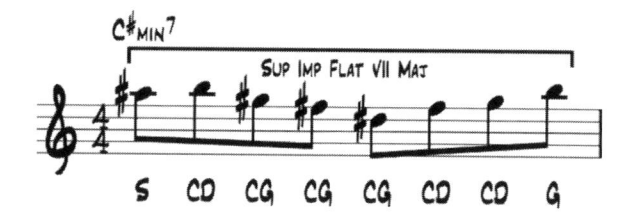

Super-Imposition on Major Triads

When super-imposing triads on a major triad many different jazz chords can be created because it opens the possibilities of the Dominant sound. In Chapter 17 and 18 the Shape Method will concentrate on those Dominant chords, but here the focus will be on major seven-quality chords.

This table lists the consonant super-impositions on a major triad.

Major Triad	Super-Imposition	Combined Tones	Resultant Chord
C Major	D Major (II)	C, D, E, F#, G, A	C 6/9 #11
C Major	E Minor (iii)	C, E, G, A, B	C Maj 7

This example demonstrates the use of the II Major Super-Imposition on a Major triad.

Chapter Summary

- The Son and Rumba Clave were discussed including strategies to correctly orient the "sides" of the Clave to the melody.

- There should be a balance between speed of harmonic rhythm and number of syncopations.

- Super-Impositions on Major and Minor chords was discussed.

Suggested Listening

On Green Dolphin Street, In A Sentimental Mood

EXERCISES

Composition Exercises

Each of the phrases, except where a Suspension or Bi-Directional Resolutions are used, should have Consonance Tones (CT, CD, or CG) on strong beats. Phrase length variance should continue to be observed. Please analyze and label each pitch the with appropriate Shape Method notation.

1) Write a two chorus solo on the following chord changes which has:

   a. Four phrases with instances of Super-Imposition on minor chords.

   b. Four phrases with instances of Super-Imposition on major chords.

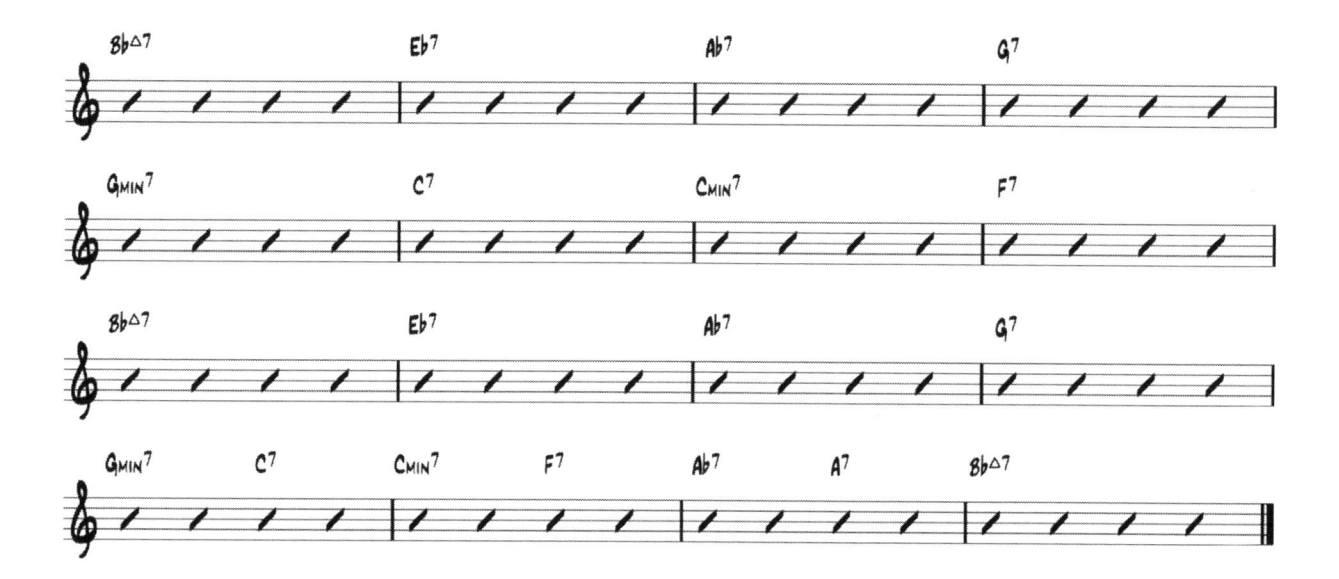

Performance Exercise

1) While tapping your foot on beats One and Three, clap the various Clave patterns; 3-2 Son, 2-3 Son, 3-2 Rumba, and 2-3 Rumba.

2) Learn and play the Super-impositions on Major and Minor triads from the tables in this chapter. (See Etude Supplement, Vol. 2)

Chapter 17 – Playing In Clave and Super-Imposition on Dominant Chords I

Playing In Clave

In Chapter 16 the Shape Method discussed the Son and Rumba Claves. Part of the discussion was how to evaluate a melody to determine how to orient the "sides" of the Clave. Correctly orienting the Clave is crucial because it needs to support the accent pattern and stasis/syncopation balance of the melody. In this chapter, the Shape Method will turn that relationship around and discuss ways to develop improvised melodies that are oriented to the Clave. Or, how to play "In Clave."

Playing "in Clave" means recognizing and working within the accent pattern of the Clave. Chapter 16 worked with performing the Clave patterns by tapping the foot on the strong beats while clapping the pattern. That is a good beginning to developing Clave, this chapter discusses how to apply melodic shape to that rhythm.

Start by playing the Consonance Tones of a chord on the articulations of the Clave. This is especially convenient because combining 1st and 2nd Order Triads on the chord generates a five-note structure, perfectly fitting the five-articulations of the Clave. The following examples are all based on a D minor 9.

The first example is Ascending and Descending Triads in 3-2 Son Clave. The remaining examples will be in 2-3 because it is more common in contemporary latin jazz.

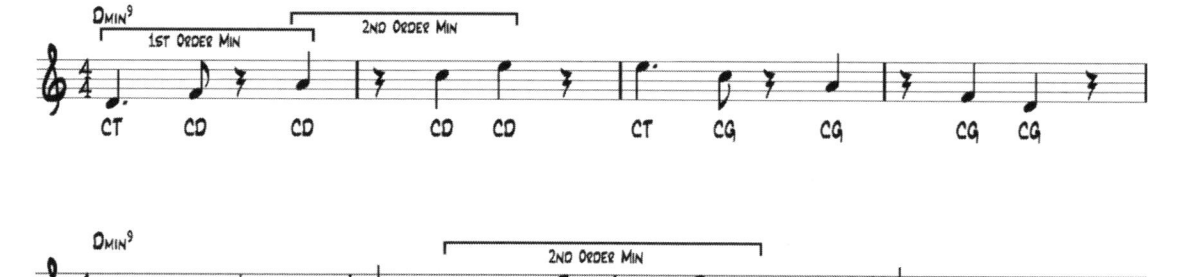

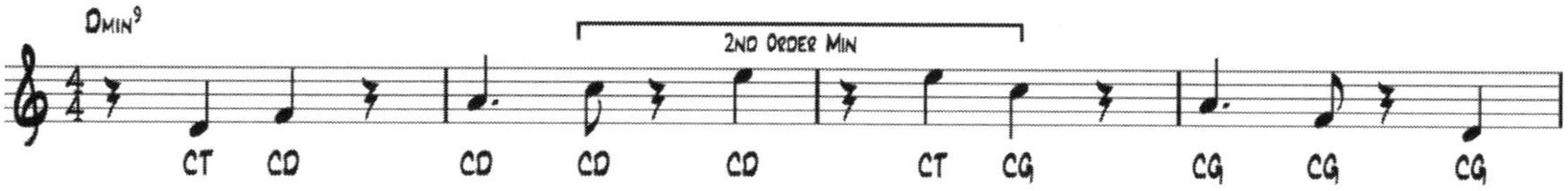

After becoming comfortable with playing arpeggios, try changing directions by alternating Consonance Drive and Consonance Gravity Tones. Here are two examples of changing directions.

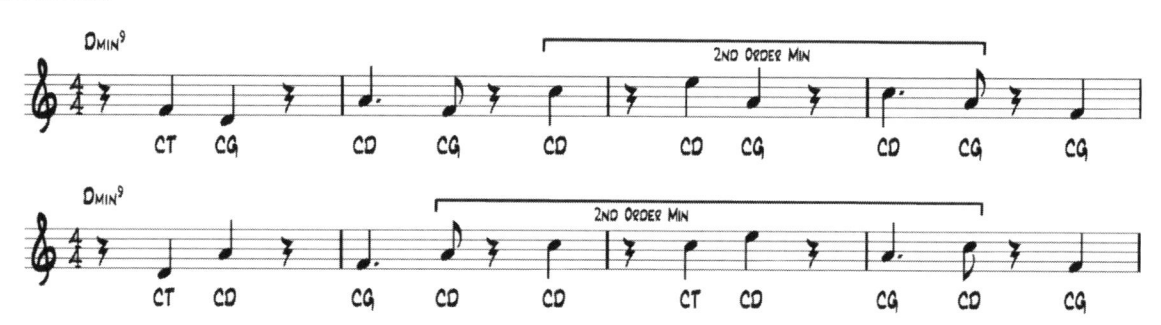

The Shape Method – Chapter 17

After changing directions of Consonance Tones becomes comfortable, start using Shape Method melodic devices to connect the accented notes. The following example uses Drive and Gravity Resolution Tones and Lower Neighbor Tones to connect the Consonance Tones used in the first 2-3 example. Note the Clave Pattern notes have accents so they can be identified more easily.

Once building melodies strictly "in Clave" has become natural, Clave vocabulary should be expanded by creating some melodies that go "against" the Clave while continuing to acknowledge it. This can be practiced by picking a beginning and ending Clave articulation and constructing a melody that begins and ends at those points. The example below demonstrates the melody starting on the second articulation of the "2-Side" of the Clave and ending on the third articulation of the "3-Side."

This practice should be expanded to longer phrase lengths to further develop rhythmic creativity while maintaining the Clave. The next example demonstrates a four-measure phrase that begins on the first articulation of the "2-Side" and stops in the fourth measure on the second articulation of the "3-Side."

While all of these examples were in Son Clave the same principles should be applied to Rumba Clave to develop a rich rhythmic palette to play "in Clave."

Super-Imposition on Dominant Chords I

Because Dominant Chords are inherently unstable, motivating resolution, there are many colorful possibilities available through Super-Imposition of Triads. The Shape Method will spend two chapters on these colors, dividing the discussion between Super-Impositions that result in Dominant Chords with a Natural 13 and those with an Augmented Fifth.

When discussing Super-Impositions, it is necessary to understand that, in almost all cases, Consonance Tones of the foundational chord are present, but only triad tones of the super-imposition. The table below lists the consonant super-impositions on a Dominant Chord.

In addition, the Resultant Chords do not have to contain all members of the chord, but represent the most likely application of the Super-Imposition in a harmonic context. While Triads based on the fifth (v) are accounted in the Shape Method as 2nd Order Triads, they are still represented here as static harmonies.

The following Dominant Chords all contain a Natural 13.

Major Triad	Super-Imposition	Combined Tones	Resultant Chord
C Major	D Major (II)	C, D, E, F#, G, A	C13#11
C Major	D Minor (ii)	C, D, E, F, G, A	C13
C Major	E Flat Major (bIII)	C, Eb, E, G, A, Bb	C7#9
C Major	E Flat Minor (biii)	C, Eb, E, Gb, G, A, Bb	C7#9#11
C Major	F Major (IV)	C, E, F, G, A	C13sus4
C Major	F Sharp Major (#IV)	C, C#, E, F#, G, A, Bb	C13b9#11
C Major	F Sharp Minor (#iv)	C, C#, E, F#, G, A	C13b9#11
C Major	G Minor (v)	C, D, E, G, A, Bb	C9
C Major	A Major (VI)	C, C#, E, G, A	C13b9
C Major	B Flat Major (bVII)	C, D, E, F, G, A, Bb	C11
C Major	B Flat Minor (bvii)	C, Db, E, F, G, A, Bb	C11b9

The Shape Method – Chapter 17

Super-Imposition on Dominant Chords is a very commonly used device and there will be several examples. However, there are two features common to almost all of these Super-Impositions:

1) The Super-Impositions frequently occur during the last two beats of the sounding of the Dominant Chord, creating additional tension directly before the resolution.

2) The Super-Impositions are motivic in nature, a brief musical figure.

Here are examples of the use of Super-Imposition on Dominant Chords that imply a Natural 13.

The first example is a Super-Imposition of a bIII, in this case Ab Major over an F7 chord.

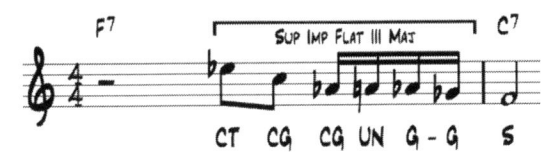

This example is a Super-Imposition of a bV, in this case Gb Major over an C7 chord.

The third example is a Super-Imposition of a VI, in this case E Major over an G7 chord.

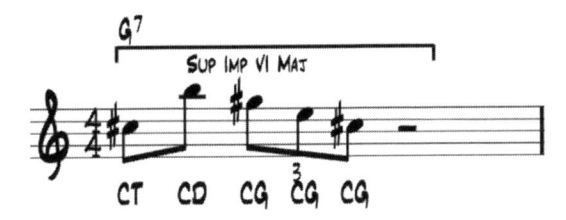

The final example is a Super-Imposition of a bVII, in this case F Major over an G7 chord. This one is not quite as easy to see because it begins on a Suspension.

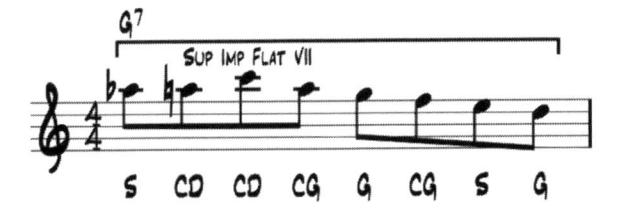

Chapter Summary

- Strategies for developing skills to play "in Clave" were discussed.
- Super-Imposition on Dominant Chords that have natural thirteenths was discussed.

Suggested Listening

There Is No Greater Love, Confirmation

The Shape Method – Chapter 17

EXERCISES

Composition Exercises

Each of the phrases, except where a Suspension or Bi-Directional Resolutions are used, should have Consonance Tones (CT, CD, or CG) on strong beats. Continue to observe the need for phrase length variance. Please analyze and label each pitch the with appropriate Shape Method notation.

1) Write two one-chorus solos on the following chord changes. The first chorus will be in 2-3 Son Clave, the second in 2-3 Rumba Clave. Make sure the phrase are "in Clave" and have.

    a. Four instances of Super-Imposition on minor chords.

    b. Four instances of Super-Imposition on dominant chords.

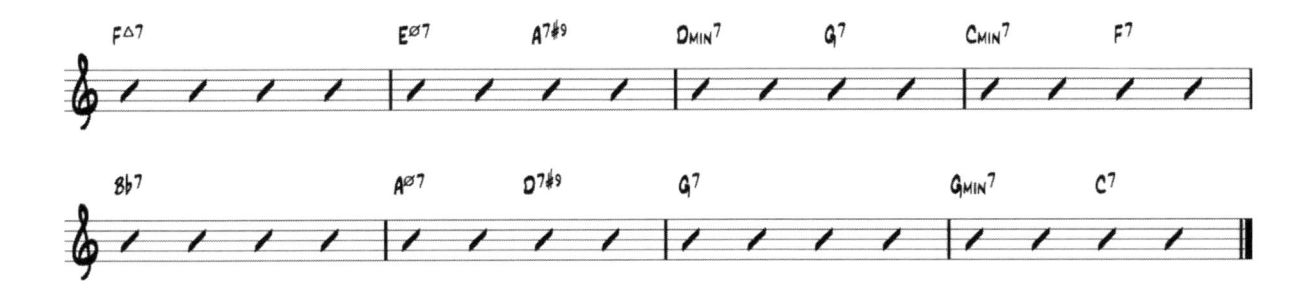

[Musical staff with chord changes:]

Line 1: F△7 | Eø7 A7♯9 | Dmin7 G7 | Cmin7 F7

Line 2: B♭7 | Aø7 D7♯9 | G7 | Gmin7 C7

Performance Exercise

1) Learn and play the Super-impositions on Dominant 13th chords from the table in this chapter. (See Etude Supplement, Vol. 2)

Chapter 18 – Cross-Metering I and Super-Imposition on Dominant Chords II

Cross-Metering I

Cross-metering is an interesting approach to creating rhythmic tension in a jazz improvisation. The Shape Method defines **Cross-Metering** as repeated groupings of accents in a pattern that contrasts the underlying meter. This chapter will address the concept of consistent metric groupings of three in a 4/4 meter context.

In the following examples the "tick marks" above the notes represent the rhythmic groupings. In the top line the rhythmic grouping represent the underlying rhythmic structure in 4/4 meter. In the lower line the tick marks represent the new rhythmic groupings of three eighth-note subdivisions. Each example ends when the rhythmic tension is ultimately released and both patterns have accents on beat one of 4/4 meter. (When cross-metering it is easy to find the rhythmic resolution by finding the Lowest Common Multiple of the number of eighth-notes being grouped and the number of eighth-notes in a measure plus one.)

This example demonstrates that when "three on four" cross-metering begins on the first beat the rhythms resolve at the fourth measure.

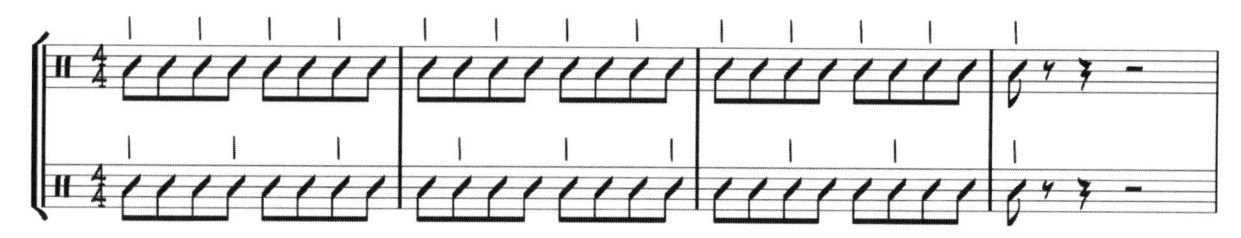

This example demonstrates the resolution of the two lines at the third measure when the "three on four" cross-metering has been shifted to the & of 1.

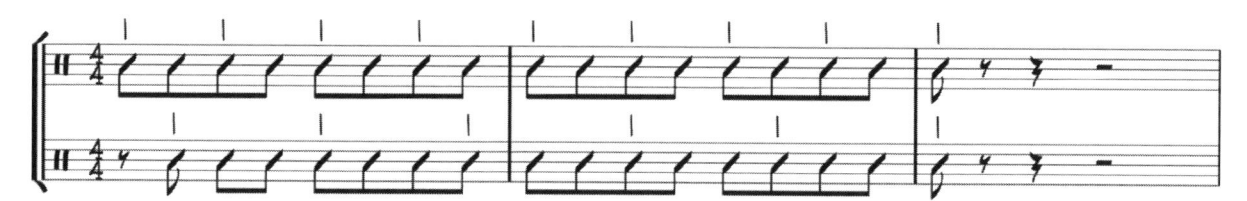

By displacing the cross-metering another eighth-note, to beat 2, this example demonstrates that the resolution comes much more quickly, on one of the next measure.

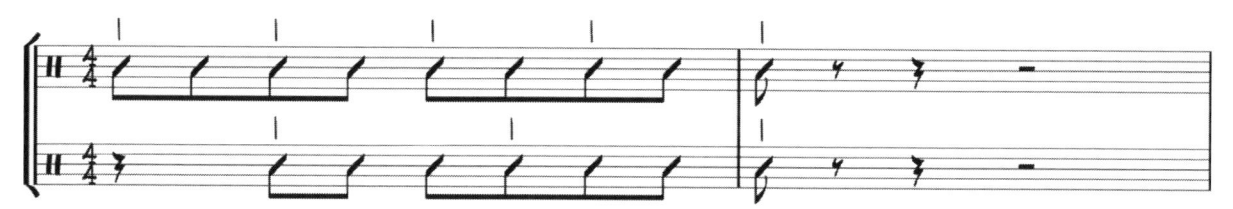

Every eighth-note displacement after that causes the cross-metering to repeat the same resolution pattern: starting on the & of 2 results in resolution on the fourth measure and starting on 3 resolves on the third measure. Starting on the & of 3 resolves immediately two the second measure, so it is considered a multiple of beat one (the same as starting on beat one because the repetition of accents doesn't begin until beat one).

Cross-metering is most easily heard when the same melodic shape is being played. The most frequent practice is to either play the same pitches or to play a sequence.

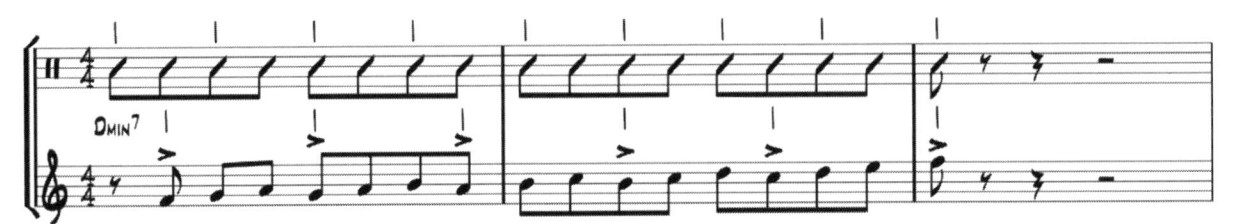

Additional rhythmic interest can be achieved by dropping out one of the notes of the cross-metered phrase. Any combination of not sounding note one, two, or three of the three-note grouping will result in interesting phrases.

Super-Imposition on Dominant Chords II

In Chapter 17 the Shape Method discussed Super-Impositions on Dominant Chords that result in Dominant Chords with a Natural 13, in this chapter those with an Augmented Fifth are addressed.

This is where one of the Shape Method definitions needs to be a little flexible. Usually, all Consonance Tones of the foundational chord are present, but because of the presence of the Augmented Fifth/Flat 13 these Super-Impositions do not consider the Sixth of the foundational triad as a Consonance Tone. Instead, the Sixth of the Super-Imposed triad becomes a Consonance Tone.

The table below lists the consonant super-impositions on a Dominant Chord. As in Chapter 17, the Resultant Chords do not have to contain all members of the chord, but represent the most likely application of the Super-Imposition in a harmonic context.

The following Dominant Chords all contain an Augmented Fifth/Flat 13.

Major Triad	Super-Imposition	Combined Tones	Resultant Chord
C Major	D Flat Major (bII)	C, Db, E, F, G, Ab, Bb	C7b911b13
C Major	D Flat Minor (bii)	C, Db, E, G, Ab, Bb	C7b9b13
C Major	F Minor (vi)	C, D, E, F, G, Ab	C7sus4b13
C Major	A Flat Major (bVI)	C, Eb, E, F, G, Ab	C7#9b13

As with Super-Impositions discussed in Chapter 17, they frequently occur during the last two beats of the sounding of the Dominant Chord, creating additional tension directly before the resolution.

The first example demonstrates an incomplete Flat II Super-Imposition, the quality of the third is unknown because it is not present.

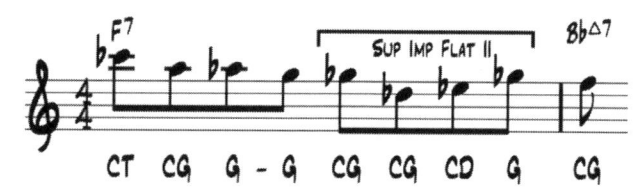

This example is a clear use of the Flat II Minor Super-Imposition, one of the most common.

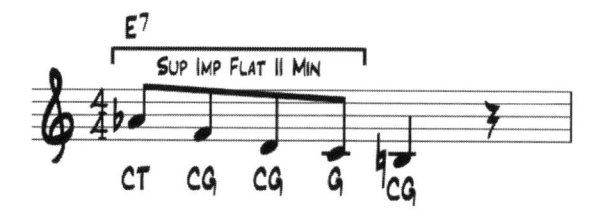

The final example is the Flat VI Major Super-Imposition.

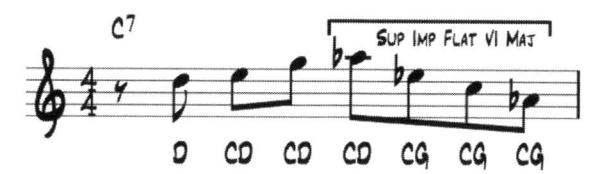

Chapter Summary

- Cross-metering by consistent metric groupings, specifically 3 eighth-notes in 4/4 meter was discussed.

- Super-Imposition on Dominant #5/b13 chords was discussed and demonstrated.

Suggested Listening

Maiden Voyage, Cantaloupe Island

EXERCISES

Composition Exercises

Each of the phrases, except where a Suspension or Bi-Directional Resolutions are used, should have Consonance Tones (CT, CD, or CG) on strong beats. Phrase length variance should continue to be maintained. Please analyze and label each pitch the with appropriate Shape Method notation.

1) Write a two chorus solo on the following chord changes in which the phrases have:

   a. Four instances of Super-Imposition on minor chords.

   b. Four instances of Super-Imposition on dominant chords.

   c. Three instances of cross-metering, one each beginning on; the & of 1, beat 3, and the & of 4.

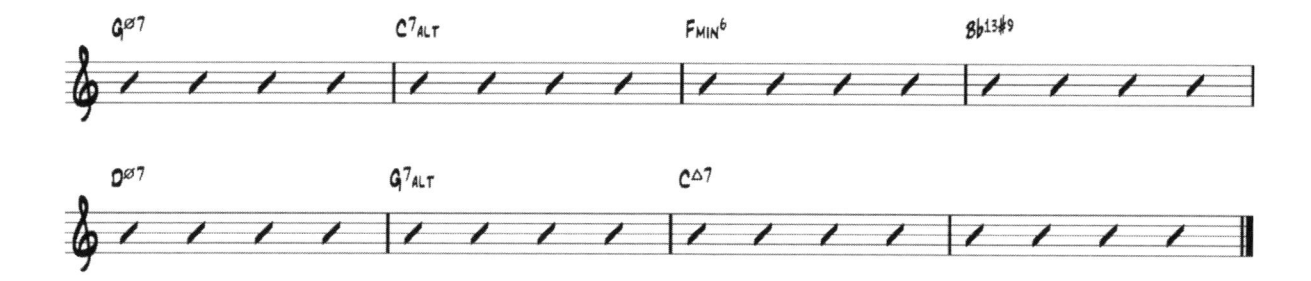

Performance Exercise

1) Learn and play the consonant Super-impositions on Dominant #5/b13 chords from the tables in this chapter. (See Etude Supplement, Vol. 2)

Chapter 19 – Cross-Metering II and Shape Stealing

Cross-Metering II

In Chapter 18 the Shape Method introduced the rhythmic technique of cross-metering. That chapter concentrated on using consistent metric groupings, groups of three in 4/4 meter. In this chapter the Shape Method will discuss varying metric groupings.

The examples below demonstrate cross-metering using varying groups of two and three pulses. Of course, these types of groups can also be displaced, creating further rhythmic interest.

This is a grouping of three pulses plus two pulses, creating a 5/8 accent pattern over the 4/4 meter. Note, the rhythmic resolution is in bar six.

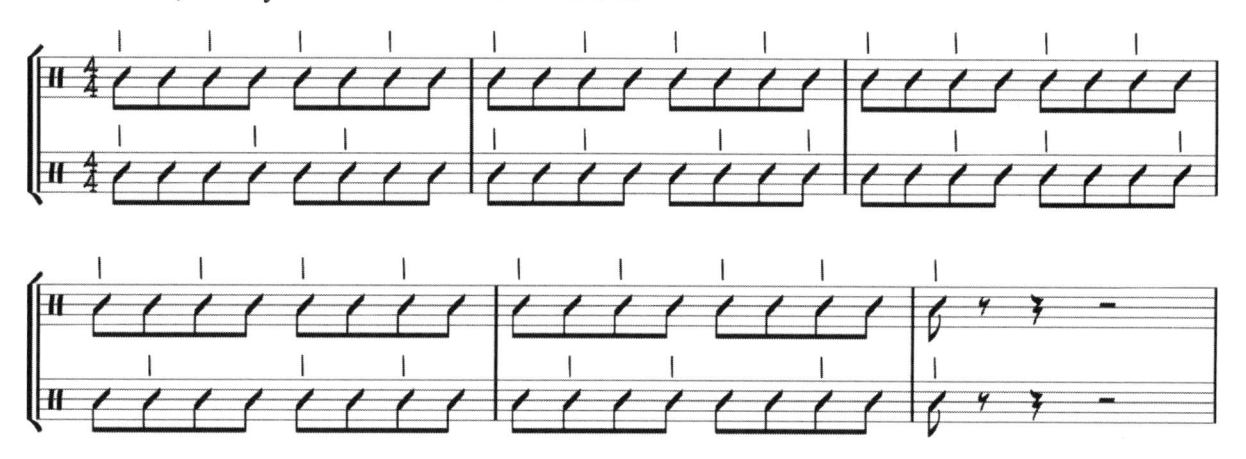

This example is a grouping of two groups of two pulses plus one group of three pulses, creating a 7/8 accent pattern over the 4/4 meter. The rhythmic resolution here is in bar eight.

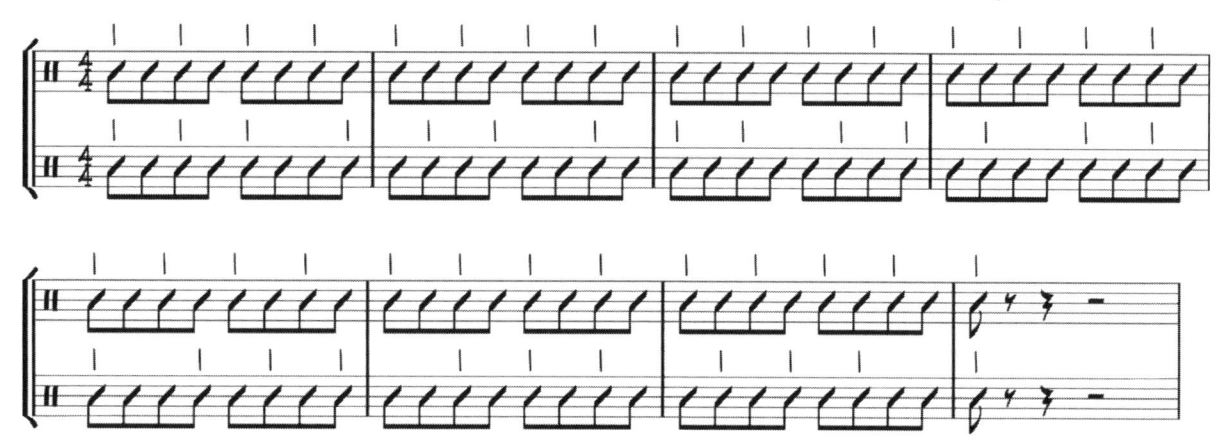

The Shape Method – Chapter 19

While it may not be appropriate to play five or seven measure-long phrases, these devices can still be used by setting a beginning and end points to a phrase. The end point will be the rhythmic resolution and the beginning point can be any one of the beginning pulse groupings. For example, in the seven-beat pattern the phrase could start on any of the following measures/beats: bar seven - & of 1, bar six – beat 2, bar 5 - & of 2, bar 4 – beat 3, bar 3 - & of 3, bar 2 – beat 4, bar 1 - & of 4 or beat 1. The accents in the lower system indicate these possible starting places.

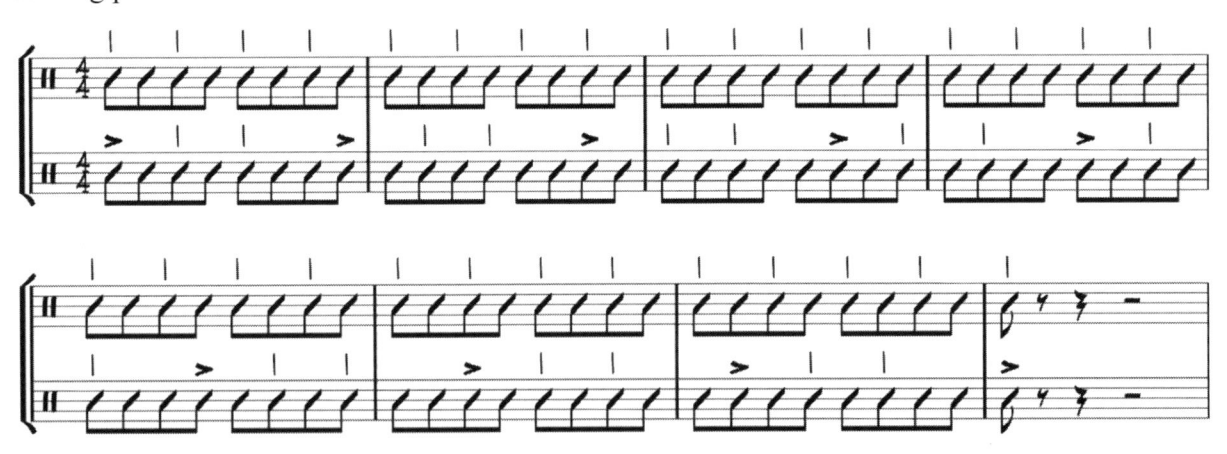

In any event, being able to sustain this type of rhythmic tension is good practice. Developing an ability to hold on to the underlying rhythmic framework while superimposing complex contrasting rhythmic figures will add further rhythmic depth and interest to improvisations.

Shape Stealing

The Shape Method's definitions of melodic tones allows for a different type of analysis that is concerned with the deeper and more universal features of a melody. Instead of being confined to a chord/scale relationship or a rigid chord tone conception of a melody, the Shape Method analysis reveals the core elements of a melody; harmonic tension/release and direction.

By understanding these two features, melodies become very portable, not just applicable to their original harmonic setting. This portability is a demonstration of just how important melodic Shape is to a great jazz improvisation. The practice of applying a melodic shape to an alternative harmonic context is called **Shape Stealing**.

The examples below are based on a popular jazz phrase. One of the characteristics of this phrase is the consistent eighth-note rhythm, and it was chosen for the example to focus on great melodic shape without the distraction of complex rhythmic information. However, melodies that have complex rhythmic shapes can also be "stolen."

The original phrase is in the harmonic area of D minor and is analyzed below.

The next examples retain the analysis and apply it to a variety of harmonic contexts <u>and</u> even use alternative Consonance Tones. The template that has been "stolen" and will be applied to other harmonies is: CT, LN, CD, D, CD, LN, CD, D, S, CD, CD, D, CD, CG, S, D, CD.

Major ii-V-I Variations

In the first variation, the harmonies are a two-measure ii-V-I in Eb Major. The first Consonance Tone is the minor third, instead of the root of the first chord.

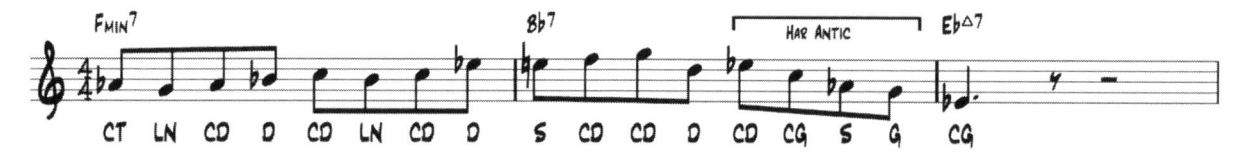

Another variation, same harmonic context, but starting with the first Consonance Tone as the sixth.

The third variation on the ii-V-I in E Flat starts the shape on the fifth of the ii chord.

Modal Variations

The next three variations demonstrate a modal application of the shape on E minor 11 resolving to A minor 11. In the first variation the shape begins on the fifth of E minor (remember, the original location was the root of a i minor chord).

The Shape Method – Chapter 19

This variation begins the shape on the root.

The third variation in this harmonic context begins on the minor third of the i minor chord.

Three-Tonic Variations

This all seems logical and self-evident, the harmonic context of the examples of been roughly similar to the original. However, the Shape Method will now demonstrate how powerful Shape Stealing can be. The next three examples take the original shape and apply it to a Three-Tonic harmonic context.

The first starts on the root of the first tonic.

The second example begins on the third of the first tonic.

The final example begins on the fifth of the first tonic.

When the shape of the phrase is strong, the application and adaption is virtually limitless.

Chapter Summary

- Cross-metering using non-consistent groups of two and three was discussed and demonstrated.
- Shape Stealing was defined and demonstrated.

Suggested Listening

26-2, Giant Steps, Countdown

The Shape Method – Chapter 19

EXERCISES

Composition Exercises

Each of the phrases, except where a Suspension or Bi-Directional Resolutions are used, should have Consonance Tones (CT, CD, or CG) on strong beats. Phrase length variance should continue to be observed. Please analyze and label each pitch the with appropriate Shape Method notation.

1) Transcribe a phrase, analyze it with the Shape Method. Write a two-chorus solo on the following changes using Shape Stealing to apply the transcribed phrase to the changes with:

   a. Two phrases starting on the Root of the chord.

   b. Two phrases starting on the Third of the chord.

   c. Two phrases starting on the Fifth of the chord.

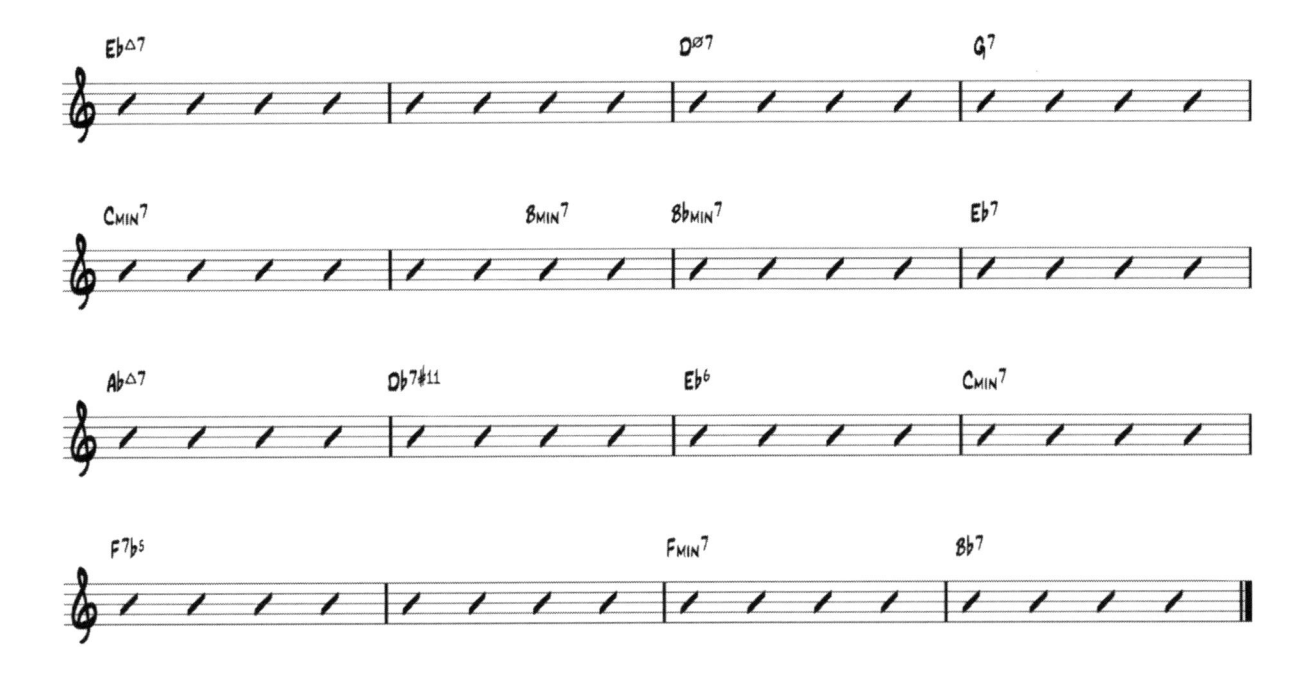

Performance Exercise

1) Play scales with 5, 7, and 9 beat accent patterns with a metronome in 4/4.

2) Shift the scales to start on different parts of the 4/4 measure.

Chapter 20 – Mixed-Meter Clave and 3rd Order Consonances

Mixed-Meter Clave

In previous chapters the Shape Method has been discussing the Clave and layering different meters over a 4/4 jazz meter. This chapter will unite those two ideas by discussing Mixed-Meter Clave.

Mixed-Meter refers to meters that are combinations of groups of two-note and three-note units to create short and long pulses. Typical meters include 5/8 or 5/4, 7/8 or 7/4, or 8/8. It is the 8/8 meter that provides the Shape Method with insight into the possibility of Mixed-Meter Clave. For the sake of brevity, the Shape Method only uses examples in 2-3 Clave. These examples can be experienced in 3-2 Clave by reversing the Sides of the Clave.

The example below demonstrates a two-measure Son Clave in 4/4 meter in the lower voice and an 8/8 meter in the upper voice with eighth-note groups. The first measure of the 8/8 phrase is a four-accent phrase grouped 2+2+2+2 and the second a three-accent phrase grouped 3+3+2.

As in Chapters 18 and 19, the tick marks indicate the groupings and the notes are also beamed to help indicate groupings.

From this two measure phrase the Shape Method extracts the basic building blocks of Mixed-Meter Claves. The first measure contains a group of four beats in which the eighth-notes are in groups of two and the Clave accents are the "2-Side."

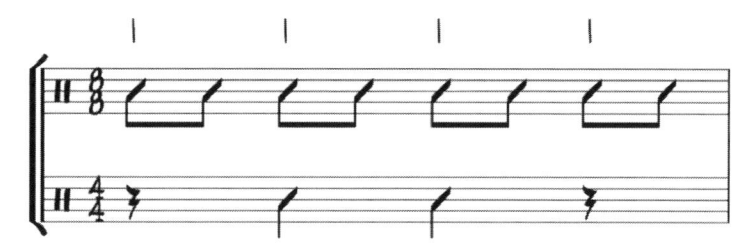

The second measure contains two components: the first three beats contain the syncopation of the Son Clave and indicate eighth-notes grouped in threes, and the final beat is a single pulse of two eighth-notes.

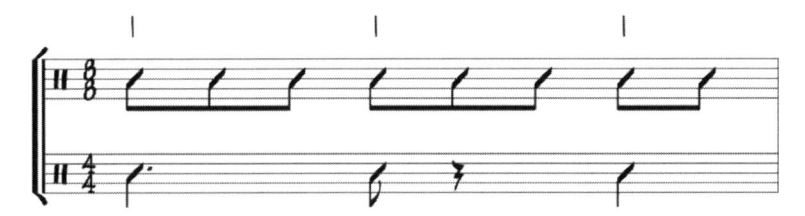

With these three components (and the Two Beat Sub-Phrase) the Shape Method can construct various Clave and quasi-Clave accent patterns to accompany Mixed-Meters. It is important to note that a *real* Clave is a five-articulation phrase that is asymmetrically divided into one side of two articulations and one side of three articulations. Some of the quasi-Clave accent patterns that will be discussed contain fewer than five and some more than five accents. However, the Clave pattern of alternating rhythmic stasis and rhythmic syncopation (or vice versa) is the feature that is retained throughout these examples.

Seven/Four Clave

This Mixed-Meter Clave in 7/4 simply trims the final articulation from the eighth beat of the two-measure pattern. This generates a Four Beat Sub-Phrase followed by a Three Beat Sub-Phrase.

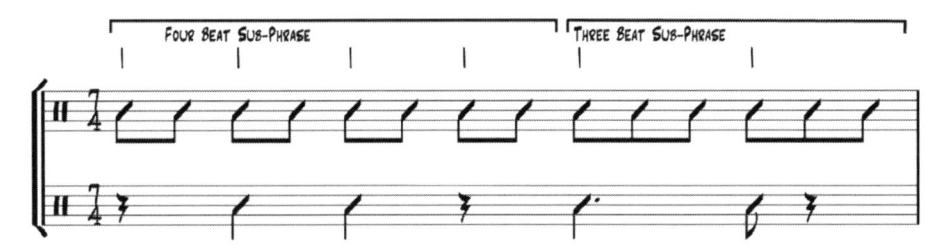

An articulation can be added to the & of 7 to generate a Rumba-esque Clave that anticipates the first beat of the repeat of the figure.

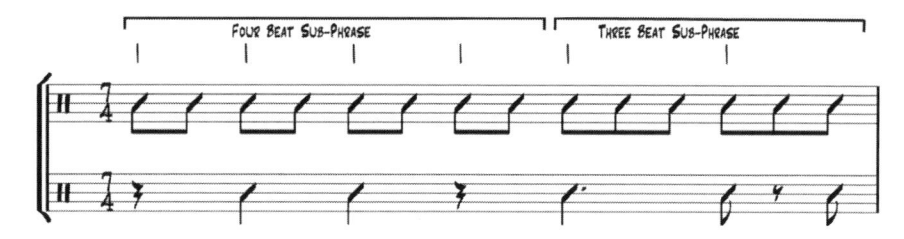

5/4 Clave

Because of a reduced number of beats, some Mixed-Meter Claves only exhibit the Clave pattern's alternating rhythmic stasis and rhythmic syncopation (or vice versa), there is no three eighth-note grouping. The 5/4 Clave below illustrates this truncated Clave-esque phrase.

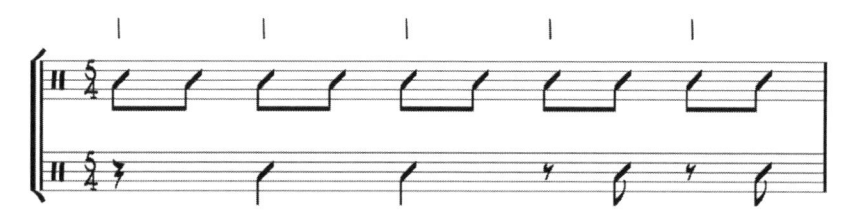

6/4 Clave

Here is another example of a truncated quasi-Clave. In 6/4 the additional beat allows for the phrase to have two "Sides."

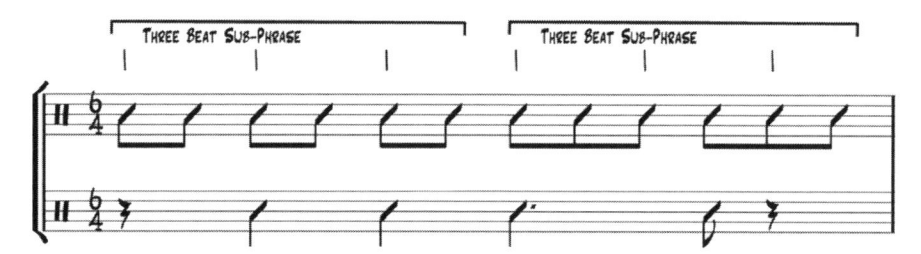

The Shape Method – Chapter 20

Longer Mixed-Meters

The following examples demonstrate ways that Sub-Phrases of Four, Three, Two, and One Beat(s) can be combined to make complex but rhythmically propulsive meters and Clave-esque patterns.

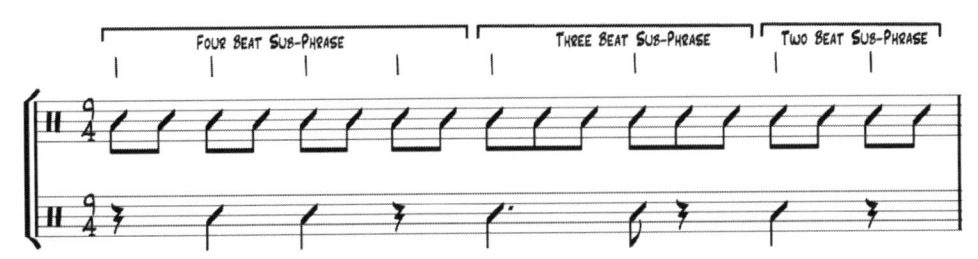

Here is another 9/4 meter with the Rumba-esque final articulation. Notice how delaying the final articulation by an eighth-note re-groups the second half of the phrase. The regrouping changes the 3+3+2+2 grouping into a 3+2+2+3 grouping and inserts a Two Beat Sub-Phrase in the middle of the Three Beat Sub-Phrase.

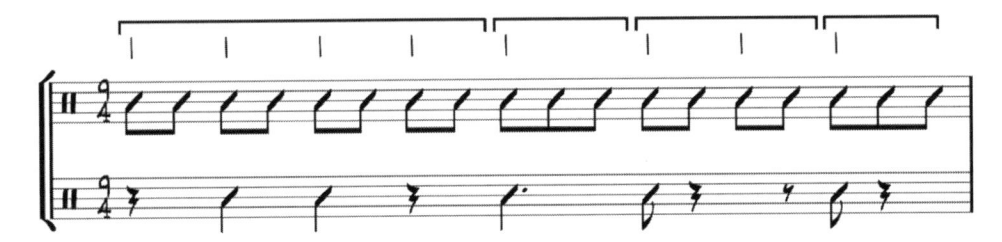

The following examples of 10/4 and 11/4 Mixed-Meters contain similar types of metric complexity.

In addition to providing interesting ways of grooving in Mixed-Meters, Clave can also provide a framework for developing interesting solo phrases. The same procedure of constructing melodies "in Clave" the Shape Method discussed in Chapter 17 can be used with Mixed-Meters.

To re-cap the procedure:

1) Play Consonance Tones on the Clave accents

2) Change directions of the Consonance Tones melody

3) Connect the Consonance Tones using Shape Method techniques

4) Pick Clave accents on which to begin and end melodies

5) Expand the phrase lengths.

Because Clave and quasi-Clave accents are not the basis of Mixed-Meters but instead are providing a potential framework, they can be further manipulated. The next two examples are rhythmic displacements of the original 7/4 Clave. The first two displaced by a quarter-note to beat one.

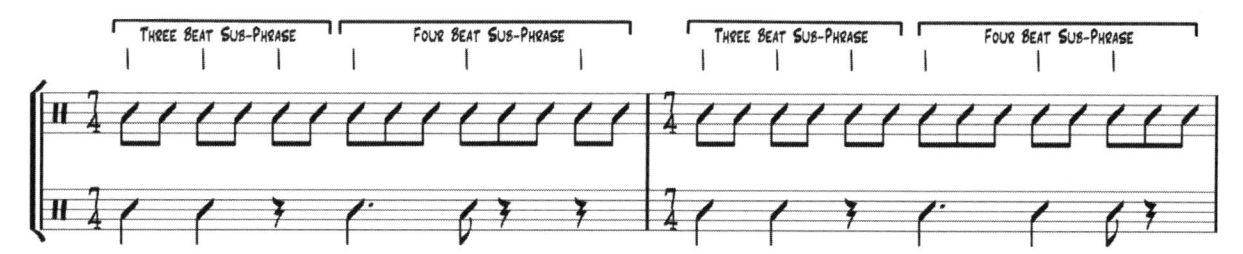

The next two displaced by an eighth-note to the & of one.

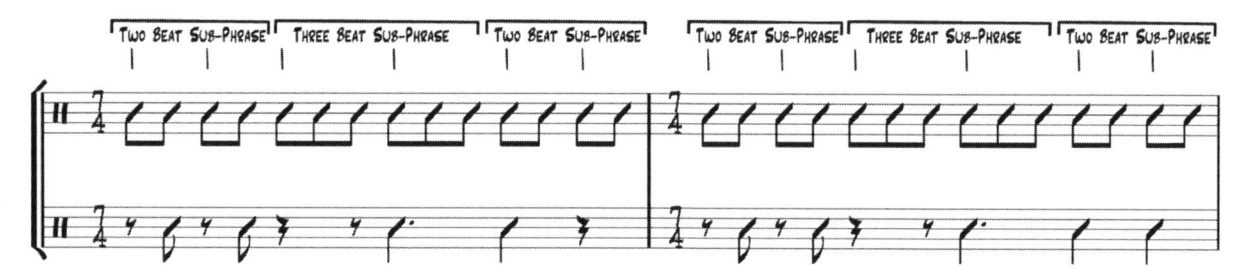

Improvisers can now apply the "Playing In Clave" melodic development techniques to these accent patterns to achieve richer rhythmic control and vocabulary.

The Shape Method – Chapter 20

3rd Order Consonances

The Shape Method defines 3rd Order Consonances as the diatonic ninth, eleventh, and thirteenth of the chord. Charlie Parker is said to have discovered a new way of playing, when he discovered he could play on "the top part of the chords." He was talking about what the Shape Method refers to as the 2nd and 3rd Order Consonances. In many ways 3rd Order Consonances are indistinguishable from super-impositions of the ii or II chord.

The next examples demonstrate some usages of 3rd Order Consonances in jazz improvisations.

The first is an example of 3rd Order Consonances as part of a descending arpeggio sequence.

This example is a brief excursion to the 3rd Order Consonance that might also be interpreted as a Harmonic Delay of the 2nd Order Consonance of the A minor 7 chord.

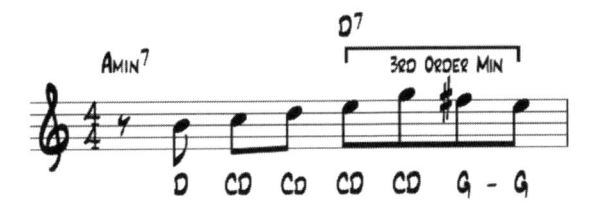

This example clearly demonstrates a D minor arpeggio (the 3rd Order Consonance Triad) on a C minor 7 chord.

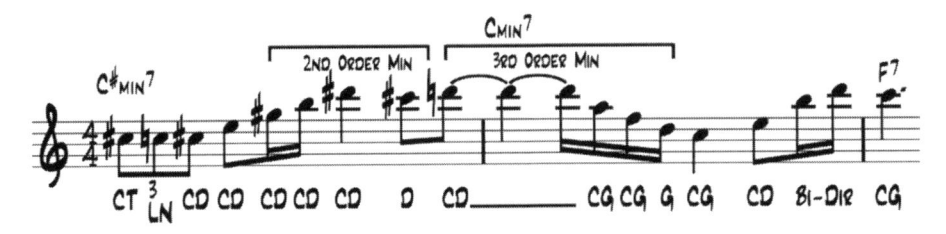

Similarly, the final example is an arpeggio of the Consonance Tones of E minor, the 3rd Order Minor Consonances of the D7 chord.

3rd Order Consonances are usually played without the use of Shape Method techniques of Resolution Tones or Suspensions when improvising on compositions with rapid harmonic movement (greater than a chord change every two measures). This is because 3rd Order Consonances are frequently heard as suspensions above 1st Order Consonances. However, the use of Shape Method melodic devices on 3rd Order Triads is fairly common when improvising on static harmonics frequently found in Contemporary Jazz.

Chapter Summary

- Mixed-Meter Clave was defined and discussed
- Developing phrases in Mixed-Meter was discussed
- 3rd Order Consonances were discussed and demonstrated.

Suggested Listening

Witch Hunt, Meeting of the Spirits, You Know, You Know, Dance of Maya

The Shape Method – Chapter 20

EXERCISES

Composition Exercises

Each of the phrases, except where a Suspension or Bi-Directional Resolutions are used, should have Consonance Tones (CT, CD, or CG) on strong beats. Phrase length variance should continue to be observed. Please analyze and label each pitch the with appropriate Shape Method notation.

1) Write "in Clave" phrases of four measures on a D minor 9 chord using the following mixed meters by first creating a Clave, then a melody:

    a. 6/4

    b. 7/4

    c. 9/4

2) Write a one chorus solo on the following changes that uses 3rd Order Consonance materials.

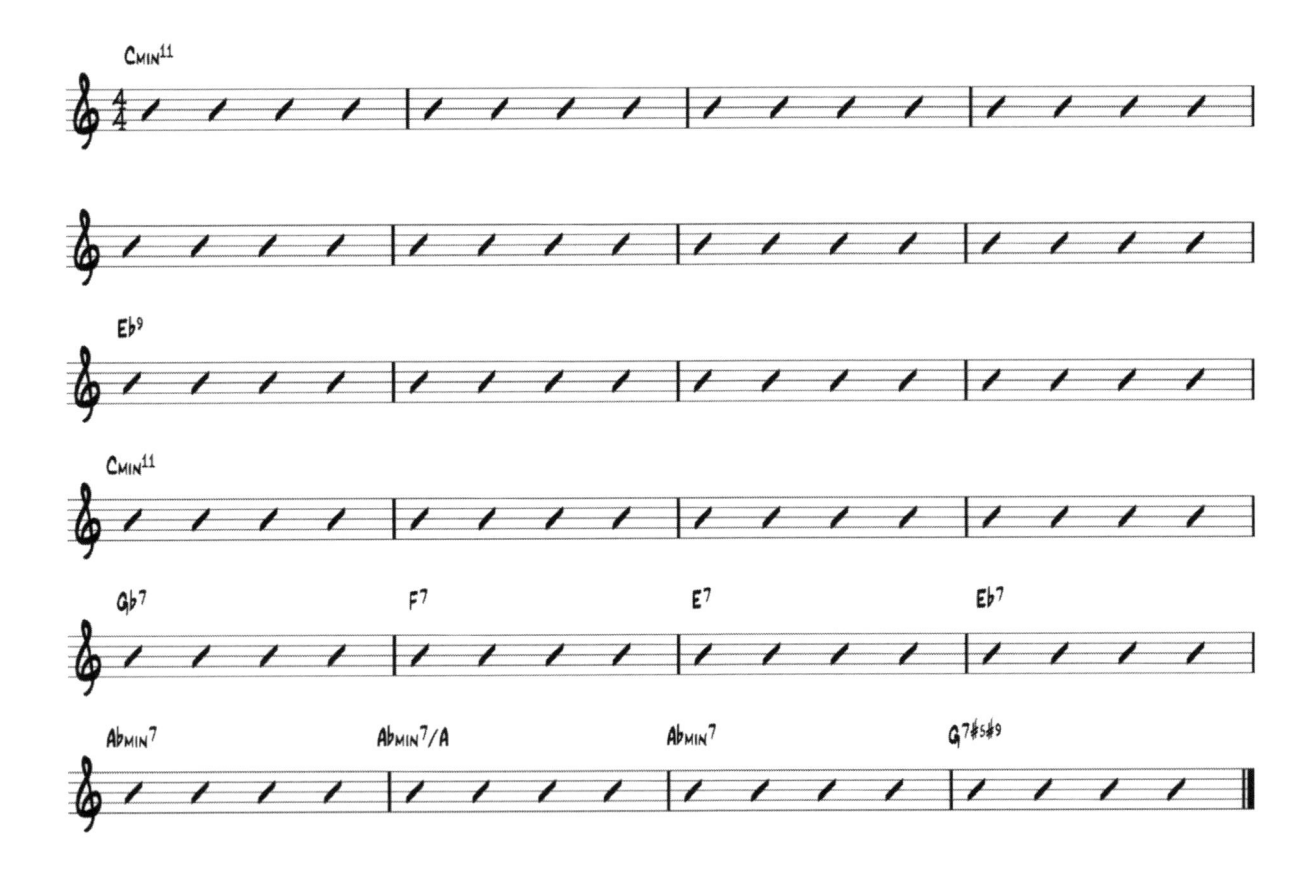

Performance Exercise

1) Learn and play the 1st, 2nd, and 3rd Order Consonances on Major and Minor triads.

Chapter 21 – Metric Modulation I and Extracting Quartal Materials From Super-Impositions and Shifting

Metric Modulations I – Eighth-Note/Triplet Sub-Division

In previous chapters the Shape Method has discussed the metric elements of super-imposing meters and mixed-meters. The next two chapters will focus on techniques to change the tempo of the underlying pulse – Metric Modulation.

The Shape Method defines **Metric Modulation** as a technique to change the tempo of the pulse via a common rhythmic division or grouping. This means there must be a common division or group between the two meters and the meaning of that division or group will change at the metric modulation, altering the pulse. This chapter will discuss the relationship between eighth-notes and triplets.

The formula for determining values of a metric modulation is very clear-cut:

> The New Tempo divided by the Old Tempo is equal to the Old Number of Units (Divisions/Groups) Per Beat/Measure divided by the New Number of Units (Divisions/Group) Per Beat/Measure.

$$\frac{NT}{OT} = \frac{OU}{NU}$$

Here the Shape Method applies the formula to find a new tempo based on jazz triplet divisions.

- Jazz tempo of 120 bpm, therefore OT = 120
- The New Unit (Grouping) will be two eighth-notes per beat, therefore NU = 2
- The Old Unit (Grouping) has three eighth-note triplets per beat (jazz feel has an implication of three triplet divisions per beat), therefore OU = 3

$$\frac{NT}{120} = \frac{3}{2}$$

$$120 \cdot \frac{NT}{120} = \frac{3}{2} \cdot 120$$

$$NT = \frac{360}{2}$$

$$NT = 180$$

The New Tempo is 180 bpm.

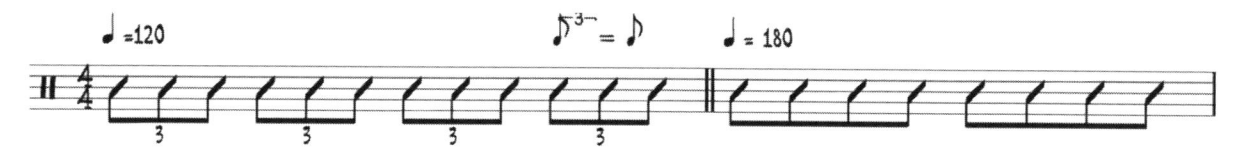

To modulate back to the original tempo the relationship of Units must be reversed. The New Tempo will now have two eighth-notes in the time the Old Tempo had two. Therefore the formula is now:

$$\frac{NT}{180} = \frac{2}{3}$$

$$180 \cdot \frac{x}{180} = \frac{2}{3} \cdot 180$$

$$NT = \frac{360}{3}$$

$$NT = 120$$

In both these examples the small division (triplet/eighth and eighth/triplet) stays the same and the pulse changes. This practice can be expanded to different rhythmic units to generate extremely complex modulations.

Extracting Quartal Materials From Super-Impositions

Because the Shape Method is primarily focused on triadic materials it is not immediately obvious how contemporary Quartal sounds could be included. However, Quartal materials can be easily generated through Super-Impositions. The following examples demonstrate how super-imposing triads can create a scale that contains sets of Quartal materials.

Because Quartal shapes are symmetrical and without a strong resolution preference they are very flexible. One of the most common practices with these materials is to shift them up or down a half step on the weak beats to create and resolve harmonic tension.

The Shape Method defines Shifts in two ways. A **Gravity Shift** transposes a figure <u>up</u> a half-step from its original pitch location, so the figure may <u>resolve</u> down. A **Drive Shift** transposes a figure <u>down</u> a half-step from its original pitch location, so the figure may <u>resolve</u> up.

The following examples demonstrate how Quartal materials can undergo Gravity and Drive Shifts and resolve.

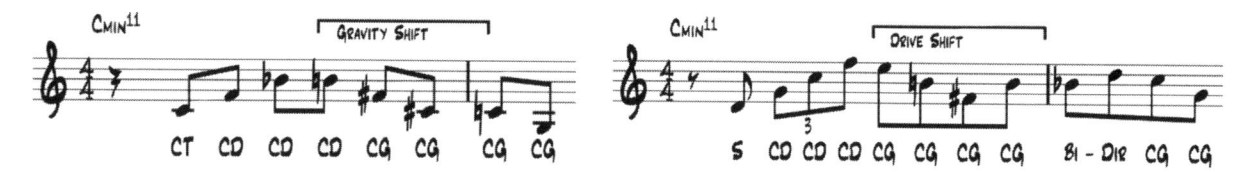

Consonance Tones frequently have Shift applied to them in contemporary jazz improvisations.

The next example demonstrates that practice.

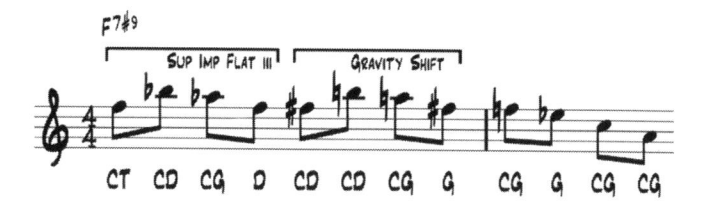

The following example demonstrates consecutive Gravity Shifts applied to Consonance Tones. Note, these are all Gravity Shifts because the shifted material is always resolving to the original from above.

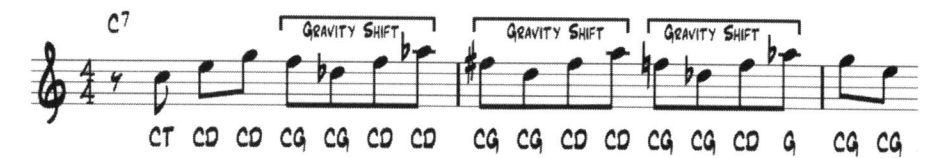

Finally, this example demonstrates mixing of Gravity and Drive Shifts.

Chapter Summary

- Metric Modulation using a common pulse division was discussed and demonstrated.
- Quartal melodic materials were created by super-imposing triads.
- Drive and Gravity Shifting was defined and demonstrated.

Suggested Listening

Freedom Jazz Dance, Mahjong, E.S.P.

EXERCISES

Composition Exercises

Each of the phrases, except where a Suspension, Bi-Directional Resolution, or Shifts are used, should have Consonance Tones (CT, CD, or CG) on strong beats. Phrase length variance should continue to be observed. Please analyze and label each pitch the with appropriate Shape Method notation.

1) Write a sixteen-measure melody that includes triplets and uses them as a metric modulation device, and then modulate back to the original tempo.

2) Write a one chorus solo on the following changes that uses Drive and Gravity Shifts.

[Chord changes over seven systems in 4/4:

System 1: F7sus | Eb6/9 | F7sus | Eb6/9
System 2: F7sus | Eb6/9 | F7sus | Eb6/9
System 3: Db△13 | Eb6/9 | Db△13 | Eb6/9
System 4: Db△13 | Eb6/9 | Db△13 | Eb6/9
System 5: D7#9 | EbMIN7 Ab7b9 | Db△9 | C#MIN7 F#13
System 6: F7sus | Eb6/9 | F7sus | Eb6/9
System 7: F7sus | Eb6/9 | F7sus | Eb6/9]

Performance Exercise

1) Practice improvising on a set of two 4ths – 1, 4, b7 and 2, 5, 1. Apply Gravity Shifts on beats 3 and 4 and resolve on beat 1. Then apply Drive Shifts on beats 3 and 4 and resolve on beat 1.

Chapter 22 – Metric Modulation II and Diminished Four-Tonic System

Metric Modulations II – Meta Pulse Modulations

In the previous chapter the Shape Method discussed metric modulation where the speed of the division of the pulse stayed the same and the rate of pulse changed. In this chapter the Shape Method discusses the converse modulation – where the large pulse rate is retained, but the divisions of the pulse are altered.

The formula for determining values of a metric modulation is similar to the formula from Chapter 21. However, in this case the goal is to find the value of the divisions and therefore the right-hand side of the equation is inverted (the reciprocal):

> The New Tempo divided by the Old Tempo is equal to the New Number of Units (Divisions/Groups) Per Beat/Measure divided by the Old Number of Units (Divisions/Group) Per Beat/Measure.

$$\frac{NT}{OT} = \frac{NU}{OU}$$

Here the Shape Method applies the formula to find the new tempo when the Half-Note pulse of 4/4 time becomes the Dotted-Half pulse of 3/4.

- Jazz of 120 bpm, therefore $OT = 120$
- The New Unit (Grouping) will be Three Quarter-Notes per measure therefore $NU = 3$
- The Old Unit (Grouping) uses Two Quarter-Notes per pulse, therefore $OU = 2$

$$\frac{NT}{120} = \frac{3}{2}$$

$$120 \cdot \frac{NT}{120} = \frac{3}{2} \cdot 120$$

$$NT = \frac{360}{2}$$

$$NT = 180$$

The New Tempo is 180 bpm per Quarter-Note.

Returning to the Old Tempo is quite easy because the Meta Pulse is the same. We simply sustain the Dotted-Half pulse and divide it into two equal pieces instead of three. This generates the original Quarter-Note tempo of 120. The math looks like this:

$$\frac{NT}{OT} = \frac{NU}{OU}$$

$$\frac{NT}{180} = \frac{2}{3}$$

$$180 \cdot \frac{NT}{180} = \frac{2}{3} \cdot 180$$

$$NT = \frac{360}{3}$$

$$NT = 120$$

Other Meta Pulses can also be generated from within meters and those can be used as metric modulation points. This is the type of modulation heard in *Blue Rondo A La Turk* as the 9/8 moves to the 4/4 Blues section.

In the example below, the original 4/4 phrase is pulsed in 2/8, 3/8, 3/8 at a Quarter-Note tempo of 102 bpm. At this tempo the speed of the Eighth-Notes is 204 bpm. There are three Eight-Notes in each 3/8 pulse and therefore the Meta Pulse speed is Dotted-Quarter at 68 bpm.

Quarter = 102

Eighth = 204

$$Dotted - Quarter = \frac{204}{3}$$

Dotted – Quarter = 68

By maintaining the Meta Pulse a Metric Modulation to 68 bpm can be accomplished.

The return to the original tempo is very similar to the methods used in Chapter 21. To modulate back to the original tempo the relationship of Units must be reversed. The New Tempo will now have two eighth-notes in the time the Old Tempo had two. Therefore the formula is now:

$$\frac{NT}{OT} = \frac{OU}{NU}$$

$$\frac{NT}{68} = \frac{3}{2}$$

$$68 \cdot \frac{NT}{68} = \frac{3}{2} \cdot 68$$

$$NT = \frac{204}{2}$$

$$NT = 102$$

Complex Meta Pulse modulations can be constructed by creating Meta Pulses of any length within meters and using those pulses as Metric Modulation devices.

The Shape Method – Chapter 22

Diminished Four Tonic System

The Shape Method has discussed Super-Impositions in a number of chapters and the technique has demonstrated its usefulness in many situations. However, the discussions have been limited to Super-Imposing one triad over another. In the final two chapters the Shape Method will address multiple Super-Impositions to create powerful and colorful sonorities and melodies.

The important consideration of multiple Super-Impositions is their symmetry. This chapter will focus on Super-Imposing three additional triads to develop diminished structures and a Four Tonic harmonic system.

When Super-Imposing either Major OR Minor Triads with roots a minor third apart create a symmetrical structure. Because the structure is symmetrical it can be started on any of the four triad roots. The following examples detail these structures in arpeggio. Notice there are only three sets.

Major Triads

The next example demonstrates the structures created when super-imposing Minor Triads.

These sounds are applicable to any Dominant 7 chord with a Natural 13 and an altered 9. They can be applied on chords that have a root on any of the four tonics in the system. They can also be used on Diminished 7 chords. Any Shape Method melodic techniques can be applied to these structures and major and minor triads can be mixed within a line because the sonority always contains both types of triads.

The three examples below demonstrate the use of these Diminished Four Tonic structures on Dominant 13 #9 chords.

The first example demonstrates super-imposing the VI and Flat iii.

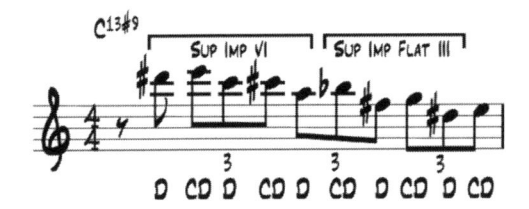

This example demonstrates an intervallic structure that is transposed down by minor thirds.

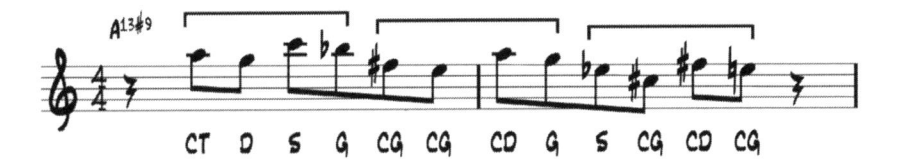

The final example demonstrates a more linear approach to using Diminished Four Tonic Super-Impositions.

Chapter Summary

- Complex Metric Modulations involving Meta Pulses was discussed and demonstrated.
- Diminished Four Tonic Systems were defined and demonstrated.

Suggested Listening

Freedom Jazz Dance

EXERCISES

Composition Exercises

Each of the phrases, except where a Suspension or Bi-Directional Resolutions are used, should have Consonance Tones (CT, CD, or CG) on strong beats. Please analyze and label each pitch the with appropriate Shape Method notation.

1) Write a sixteen-measure melody that uses Meta Pulses as a metric modulation device, and then modulate back to the original tempo.

2) Write a 16 measure solo on the following a Bb7#9 vamp at 104 bpm that uses Diminished Four Tonic Super-Impositions.

Performance Exercise

1) Learn and play the Diminished Four Tonic Super-Imposition examples in all keys. (See Etude Supplement, Vol. 2)

Chapter 23 – Motivic Development Through Rhythmic Augmentation and Diminution and Augmented and Whole Tone Three and Six Tonic Systems

Motivic Development Through Rhythmic Augmentation and Diminution

Rhythmic augmentation means to proportionally increase the values of all notes in a phrase. Remember, the Shape Method has defined a motive in Chapter 5 as a brief musical figure that has specific melodic and rhythmic content. The nature of the motive will determine its suitability for developing using rhythmic augmentation.

The following examples demonstrate three levels of rhythmic augmentation.

This example demonstrates rhythmic diminution.

Rhythmic augmentation and diminution can be combined with Rhythmic Displacement as described in Chapter 5 to create complicated and interesting phrases such as the example below.

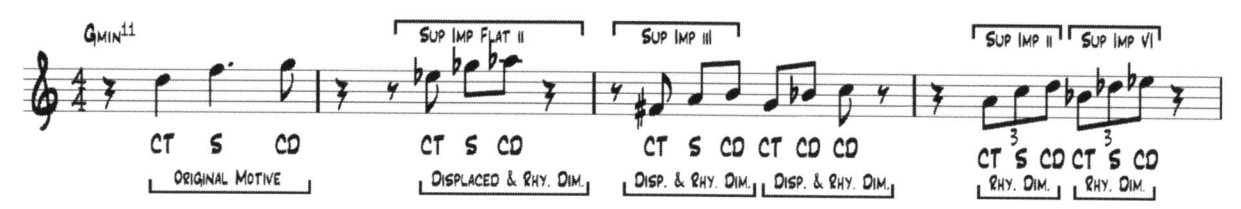

Rhythmic augmentation and diminution can be applied by any ratio. This flexibility provides a wide range of rhythmic possibilities while maintaining a connection to the underlying meter.

Augmented Three Tonic System

In Chapter 22 the Shape Method discussed multiple Super-Impositions to create a Four Tonic System. Chapter 23 discusses multiple Super-Impositions that create Three Tonic and Six Tonic Systems. The important consideration of multiple Super-Impositions remains their symmetry.

The Shape Method – Chapter 23

As with Four Tonic Systems, because the structure is symmetrical it can be started on any of the three triad roots. The following examples detail these structures in arpeggio. Notice there are only four sets.

[Musical notation: C-E-Ab Major Triads]

[Musical notation: Db-F-A Major Triads]

[Musical notation: D-F#-Bb Major Triads]

[Musical notation: Eb-G-B Major Triads]

As with Four Tonic Systems, Three Tonic Systems also contain both major and minor triads.

[Musical notation: C-E-Ab Minor Triads]

[Musical notation: Db-F-A Minor Triads]

[Musical notation: D-F#-Bb Minor Triads]

[Musical notation: Eb-G-B Minor Triads]

These Augmented Structures have a very flexible application because many Consonances Tones are possible to place on strong beats and their symmetry makes them strong and portable shapes.

The Shape Method analysis that accompanies the next two examples is in relation to the chord to demonstrate how many Consonance Tones these lines contain.

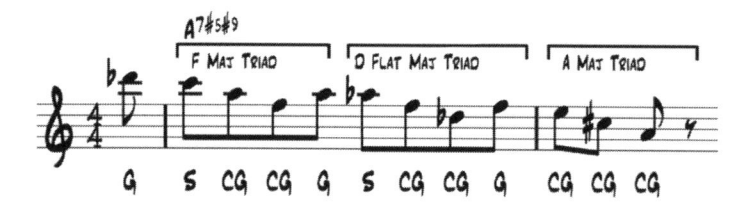

Whole Tone Six Tonic System

The Whole Tone Six Tonic System contains materials from two Augmented Systems a whole step apart.

The following examples demonstrates how the Six Tonic System can create symmetrical Bi-Directional Resolutions to Consonance Tones of an Altered Dominant chord.

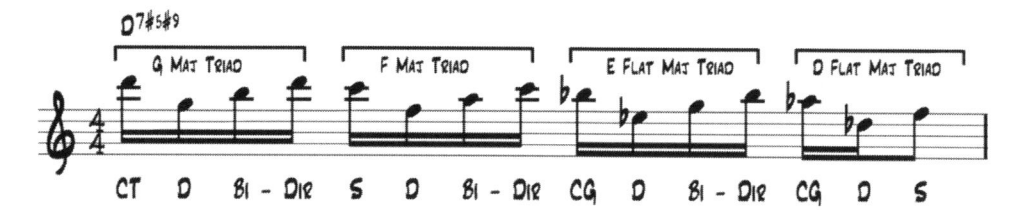

EXERCISES

Composition Exercises

Each of the phrases, except where a Suspension or Bi-Directional Resolutions are used, should have Consonance Tones (CT, CD, or CG) on strong beats. Phrase length variance should continue to be observed. Please analyze and label each pitch the with appropriate Shape Method notation.

1) Write a one chorus solo on the following chord changes which has:

   a. Two uses of Rhythmic Augmentation.

   b. Two uses of Rhythmic Diminution.

   c. Two instances of phrases that use the Three Tonic System.

   d. Two instances of phrases that use the Six Tonic System.

The Shape Method – Chapter 23

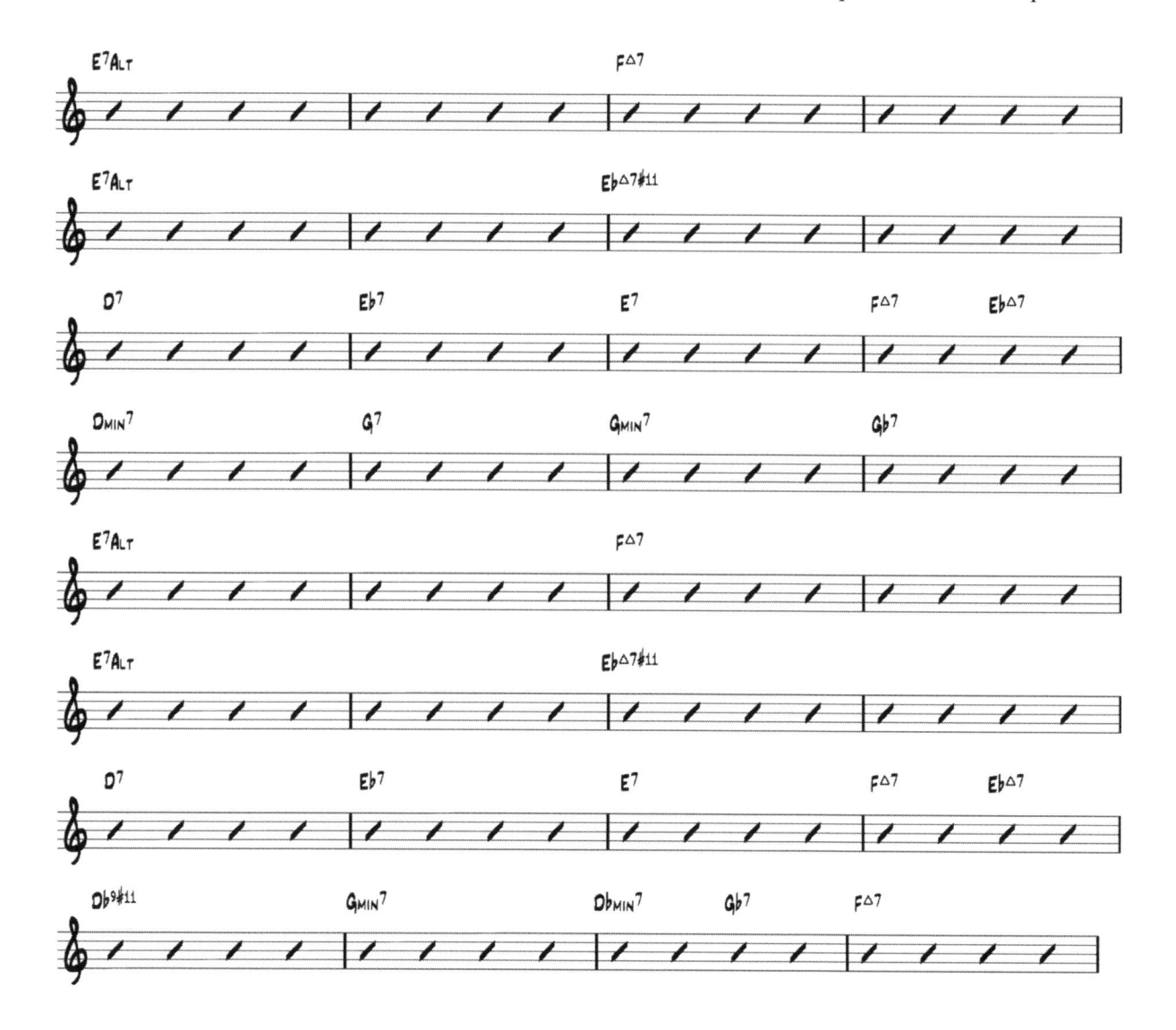

| E7ALT | | F△7 | |
| / / / / | / / / / | / / / / | / / / / |

| E7ALT | | Eb△7#11 | |
| / / / / | / / / / | / / / / | / / / / |

| D7 | Eb7 | E7 | F△7   Eb△7 |
| / / / / | / / / / | / / / / | / /   / / |

| DMIN7 | G7 | GMIN7 | Gb7 |
| / / / / | / / / / | / / / / | / / / / |

| E7ALT | | F△7 | |
| / / / / | / / / / | / / / / | / / / / |

| E7ALT | | Eb△7#11 | |
| / / / / | / / / / | / / / / | / / / / |

| D7 | Eb7 | E7 | F△7   Eb△7 |
| / / / / | / / / / | / / / / | / /   / / |

| Db9#11 | GMIN7 | DbMIN7   Gb7 | F△7 |
| / / / / | / / / / | / /   / / | / / / / |

Performance Exercise

1) Learn and play the Three and Six Tonic Super-Imposition examples that appear in this chapter. (See Etude Supplement, Vol. 2)

Glossary of Terms

When there is an abbreviation for the term it is provided in parenthesis following the term.

Anchor Phrase – A phrase in which one or more notes are repeated while a third note experiences First Degree Drive or Gravity resolutions.

Anticipation – A note that is articulated before a beat and is associated with the harmonic content of that beat.

Avoid Rhythms – Triplet rhythms that obscure the pulses.

Bi-Directional Resolution (Bi-Dir) - Any combination of First Degree Drive and Gravity resolutions, in either order.

Consonance Drive Tone (CD) – A Consonance Tone which has arrived via a Drive Resolution.

Consonance Escape Tones (UE) (LE) – A intervallic skip between strong beats, either up or down, missing one or more intervening CTs. 1, 3, 5 are most common, and 5 – 1 and 3 – 5, both descending are the most common.

Consonance Gravity Tone (CG) – a Consonance Tone which has arrive via a Gravity Resolution.

Consonance Tone (CT) – Major: 1, 3, 5, & 6. Minor: 1, min3, 4, 5, 6. Also designates that the phrase begins on a Consonance Tone, or the note is a directly repeated Consonance Tone.

Cross-Metering – Repeated groupings of accents in a pattern that contrasts the underlying meter.

Drive Resolution (D) – A non-Consonance Tone that occurs on a weak beat of or off the beat and push UP a whole or half step as part of the direction of the line.

Extended Bi-Directional Resolution (E-Bi-Dir) – A three note resolution that begins with a Drive or Gravity Resolution off the beat, jumps to the complimentary side of the Consonance Tone and resolves back with two more notes (usually half-steps) in the complimentary direction.

Gravity Resolution (G) – A non-Consonance Tone that occurs on a weak beat of or off the beat and push DOWN a whole or half step as part of the direction of the line.

Harmonic Anticipation (Har Antic) – A melody that indicates the new harmonic area by at least two beats (in 4/4 meter).

Harmonic Delay (Har Delay) – A melody that indicates the delay of the arrival at the new harmonic by at least two beats.

The Shape Method – Glossary of Terms

Harmonic Rhythm - the speed, measured in number of pulses, at which the harmonies change

Meta Pulse – a longer beat pulse that contains several subdivisions of the original meter, used in Metric Modulations

Metric Modulation - a technique to change the tempo of the pulse via a common rhythmic division or grouping

Micro-Resolutions – Resolutions that move at greater speed than eighth notes.

Motive – A brief musical figure that has specific melodic and rhythmic content.

Neighbor Tone (UN) (LN) – Pithes that occur off the beat, after a note sounds on the beat. "U" indicates Upper, "L" indicates Lower.

Octave Displacement (Oct D) – Moving a note of a melody to a different octave.

Orders – 1st, 2nd, and 3rd Orders apply to the three triads of a thirteenth chord. All chords are assumed to contain the possibility of extension to the thirteenth. Below are the definitions of the three Orders:

- 1st Order Consonance Tones are the root, third and fifth (of any quality) of the chord
- 2nd Order Consonance Tones are the fifth (any quality), seventh, and ninth (any quality) of the chord
- 3rd Order Consonance Tones are the ninth (any quality), eleventh (perfect or augmented), and thirteenth (major or minor) of the chord.

Re-barring - over-laying a more complex meters on the Common Time pulse.

Returning Sixteenth Micro-Resolutions – sixteenth note phrases that begin on a Consonance Tone, move away through 2nd Degree Drive or Gravity Resolutions, and then return to the initial Consonance Tone.

Returning Triplet Micro-Resolutions – triplet phrases that begin on a Consonance Tone, move away through 2nd Degree Drive or Gravity Resolutions, and then return to the initial Consonance Tone.

Sequence – direct repetition of a motive at a different pitch level.

Shape Stealing – The practice of applying a melodic shape to an alternative harmonic context.

Shift – transposing a figure up or down a half-step from its original pitch location. **Gravity Shifts** transpose the figure up then resolve down and **Drive Shifts** transpose the figure down then resolve up.

Sub-Phrase – Groupings of eighth-notes and Clave accents that imply phrases in various lengths of one, two, three, and four beats.

Super-Imposition (Sup Imp) – The superimposition of a triad other than 2nd or 3rd Order Triads.

Suspension (S) – Non-Consonance Tones that sound on the beat.

Suspension Escape Tones (UE) (LE) - Begins with a suspension then move to any note OTHER than the complimentary Bi-Directional Resolution. "U" indicates Upper, "L" indicates Lower.

Appendix I - Advanced Chord Implications of Chromatic Super-Impositions

Although the Shape Method does not address chord/scale relationships, there are some interesting static chord implications of Triad Super-Impositions. The Chord/Scale interpretations do not have to contain all members of the chord, but represent the most likely application of the Super-Imposition in a harmonic context. The asterisk indicates a common application of the Super-Imposed Triad. While Triads based on the fifth (V and v) and ninth (ii) are accounted in the Shape Method as 2nd and 3rd Order Triads, they are still represented here as static harmonies.

The following chart details interpreted chord/scales over a I Major Triad.

Root of Sup Imp	Interpreted Chord	Interpreted Scale
bII	7b911b13	5th Mode of Harmonic Minor
bii	7b9b13*	Dim-W.T.
II	13#11*	Lydian Dom. Or Lydian
ii	Dom13*	Major or Mixolydian
bIII	7#9*	H.-W. Dim
biii	7#9#11*	H.-W. Dim
III	Maj7#5*	Lydian Augmented
iii	Maj7*	Major or Lydian
IV	13sus4*	Major or Mixolydian
iv	7susb13	5th Mode of Melodic Minor

Root of Sup Imp	Interpreted Chord	Interpreted Scale
#IV	7b9#11*	H.-W. Dim
#iv	13b9#11*	H.-W. Dim
V	Maj9*	Major or Lydian
v	9*	Mixolydian
bVI	7#9b13*	Dim-W.T.
bvi	minMaj7#5	Augmented
VI	13b9*	H.-W. Dim
vi	6*	Major or Lydian
bVII	Dom11*	Mixolydian
bvii	11b9*	5th Mode of Harmonic Minor
VII	Dim7*	6th Mode of Harmonic Minor
vii	Maj9#11*	Lydian

The Shape Method – Appendix I

The following chart details interpreted chord/scales over a i Minor Triad.

Root of Sup Imp	Interpreted Chord	Interpreted Scale
bII	m7sus4b9b13	Phrygian*
bii	7b9#9b13	Spanish Phrygian*
II	7#11	Blues Maj6
ii	min713*	Dorian
bIII	min7*	Dorian
biii	M7#11	Blues min7
III	M7#5	Augmented
iii	Maj7#9	Augmented
IV	min13	Dorian
iv	min711b13	Aeolian

Root of Sup Imp	Interpreted Chord	Interpreted Scale
#IV	7b9#11*	H.-W. Dim
#iv	13b9#11*	H.-W. Dim
V	minMaj9*	Melodic Minor
v	min9*	Dorian
bVI	m7b13	Aeolian*
bvi	minMaj7b6	Harmonic Minor
VI	13b9	H.-W. Dim*
vi	13	6th Mode of Harmonic Minor
bVII	min11*	Dorian
bvii	m7b9	Phrygian*
VII	minMaj9#11	W.-H. Dim
vii	minMaj11	W.-H. Dim

Appendix II – Why The Blues Scale Works

The Shape Method doesn't discuss scales, except in the previous appendix, purposefully avoids chord/scale relationships. However, there is one important scale-related issue that is related to the Shape Method concepts of Consonance, Resolution, and Melodic direction – the Blues Scale.

Because the sound of the tonic of the Blues is a often a dominant chord, a wide variety of colors are available. The most common of those colors is the Sharp 9 on the Dominant I chord, but there are others. The IV chord is also a Dominant quality and many times the Flat 9 is heard on that chord, and the Dominant V chord frequently includes the Sharp 5 and the Sharp 9.

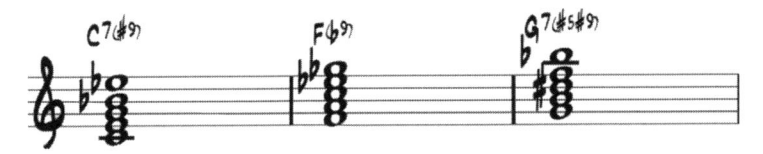

When these chord tones are taken together they form the following composite.

The following composite pitches arranged in a linear fashion could be interpreted as a scale. In fact, they are one of the "Blues Scales." The example below demonstrates the most common Blues Scale.

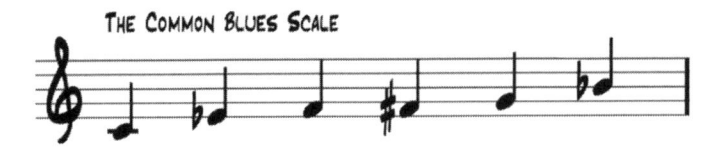

The Shape Method proposes another scale that is drawn from the concept of Consonance Tones. Since the tonic of the Blues is a V7(#9) the melodies created in that environment are often a minor quality, the Shape Method begins with the Consonance Tones of the minor chord.

To this set of C minor Consonance Tones the Shape Method adds one more note, the Sharp 4. However, this tone is not new to the Consonance Tones because it is the fifth (misspelled as the Augmented four), and remember that <u>all</u> qualities of the fifth are Consonance Tones in a Dominant Chord context. Therefore, the Shape Method Blues Scale is –

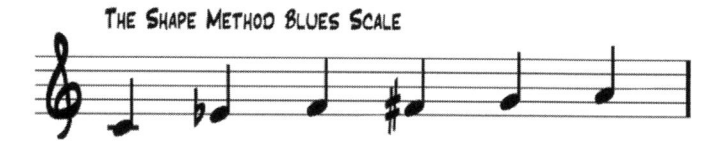

The Shape Method Blues Scale

Since Melodic Direction is such an important concept in the Shape Method it is important to mention it in this discussion. Of course, Shape Method Resolutions are applied to this scale and the chords of the blues just as they are in other chord changes. However, the Augmented 4th/Diminished 5th needs special attention with regard to melodic direction. Because that note is equidistant from the root and its octave, it acts as a pivot point in melodic direction.

If the phrase already has an ascending character, the pivot note is most frequently observed as an Augmented 4th and resolves with a Drive Resolution to the Perfect 5th. If, as is more often the case, the phrase already has a descending character, the pivot note is most frequently observed as a Diminished 5th, resolving in a Gravity Resolution to the Perfect 4th.

The example below demonstrates the relationships between the Shape Method Blues Scale and the principle chords of the blues. Notice that for the F7 chord the fourth mode of the scale is used and for the G7 the fifth mode.

The relationships of the Shape Method Blues Scale to the basic chords of the blues are easy to see. Those relationships help us understand why the Blues Scales Works so well in this context. That being said, Shape Method melodic devices can still be applied to all chords of a blues to generate stylistic bebop improvisations.

The Shape Method – Appendix II

The following examples apply Shape Method analysis to several typical phrases based on the Blues Scale. The upper analysis is in relation to a C7 chord, the middle to a F7 chord, and the lower a G7 chord. Phrases on chords that have many Suspensions do not work as well as those that have more Consonance Tones.

C7#9
F7b9
G7#5#9
CT S CG CG LN CD CG CD
CT S G CG LN CD S S
S CG CG S LN S CG CD

C7#9
F7b9
G7#5#9
CT CD D CD D CD CG CD CG
CT S D CD D S CG S CG
D CG D S - S CD G S CG

C7#9
F7b9
G7#5#9
CT G CG G CG CG S CG
CT G S G CG CG S CG
S CG CG G S CG S S

C7#9
F7b9
G7#5#9
3
S CD CT CT S CD CT CT S CG LN CD CG CD CD
S S S S S S S S S CG LN CD CG S CD
S CD CT CT S CD CT CT S - S LN S CG CD S

C7#9
F7b9
G7#5#9
3
CT LN CD CT S CG S S CG LN CD CT CG LN CD CT CG CG S CD S CG CG CG LN CD
CT LN CD CT S S S S S LN S S CG LN CD CT S CG S UN S CG G CG LN CD
S LN S S CG CG CD CT CG LN CD CT S LN S S CG CG S CD S - S CG CG LN CD

The Shape Method – Appendix II

The Shape Method – Appendix III

Appendix III – Public Domain Jazz Phrases With Shape Method Analysis

There are dozens of "public domain" jazz phrases that successful jazz improvisers borrow from and adapt. The Shape Method provides some below to demonstrate the way this analysis relates to standardized fragments of the language. Note, sometimes the resolutions have to be assumed to analyze the final pitch in the measure, they may be different based on the actual musical situation.

Two Measure ii-V's

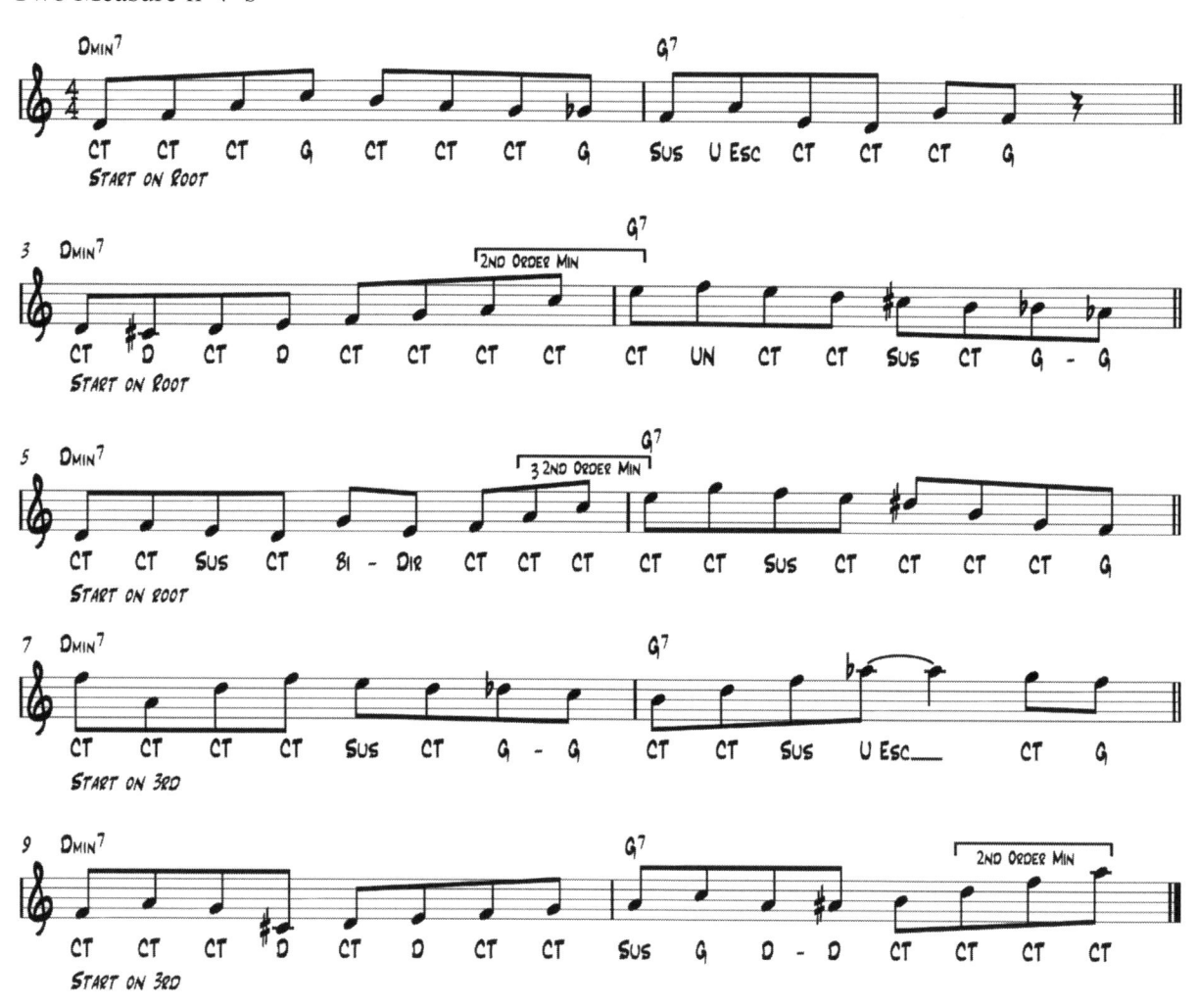

The Shape Method – Appendix III

One Measure ii-V's

The Shape Method – Appendix III

Two Measure V7Alt to i

The Shape Method – Appendix III

Two Measure iii – vi – ii – V7

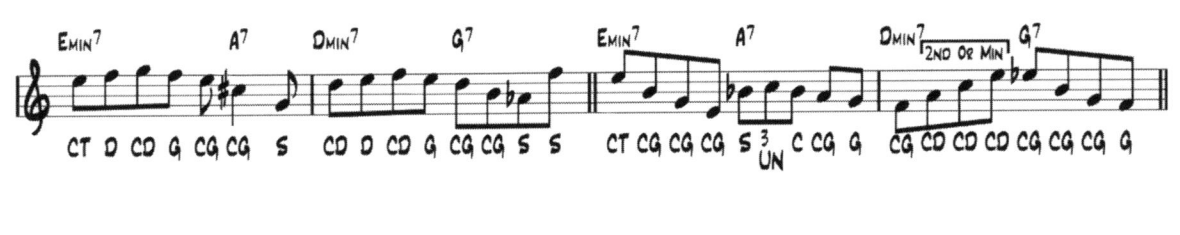

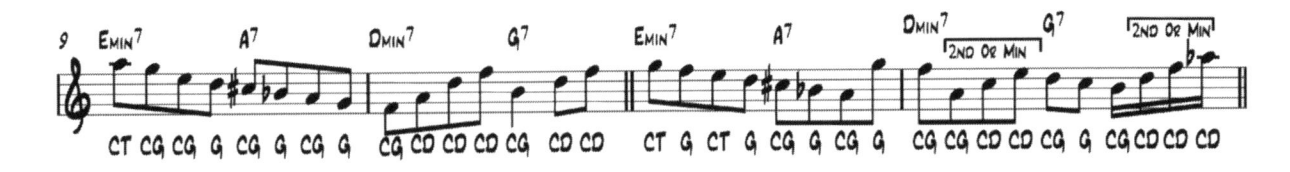

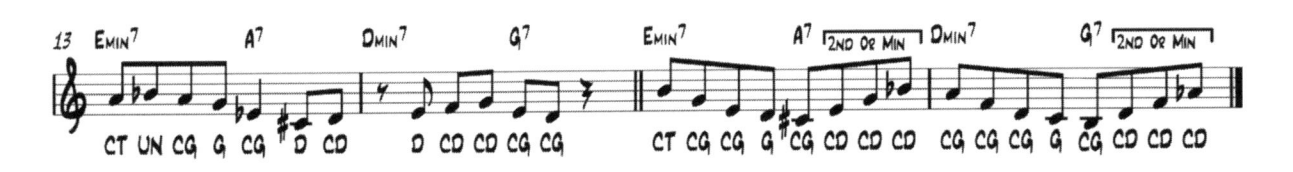

The Shape Method – Appendix III

One Measure Cycle Patterns

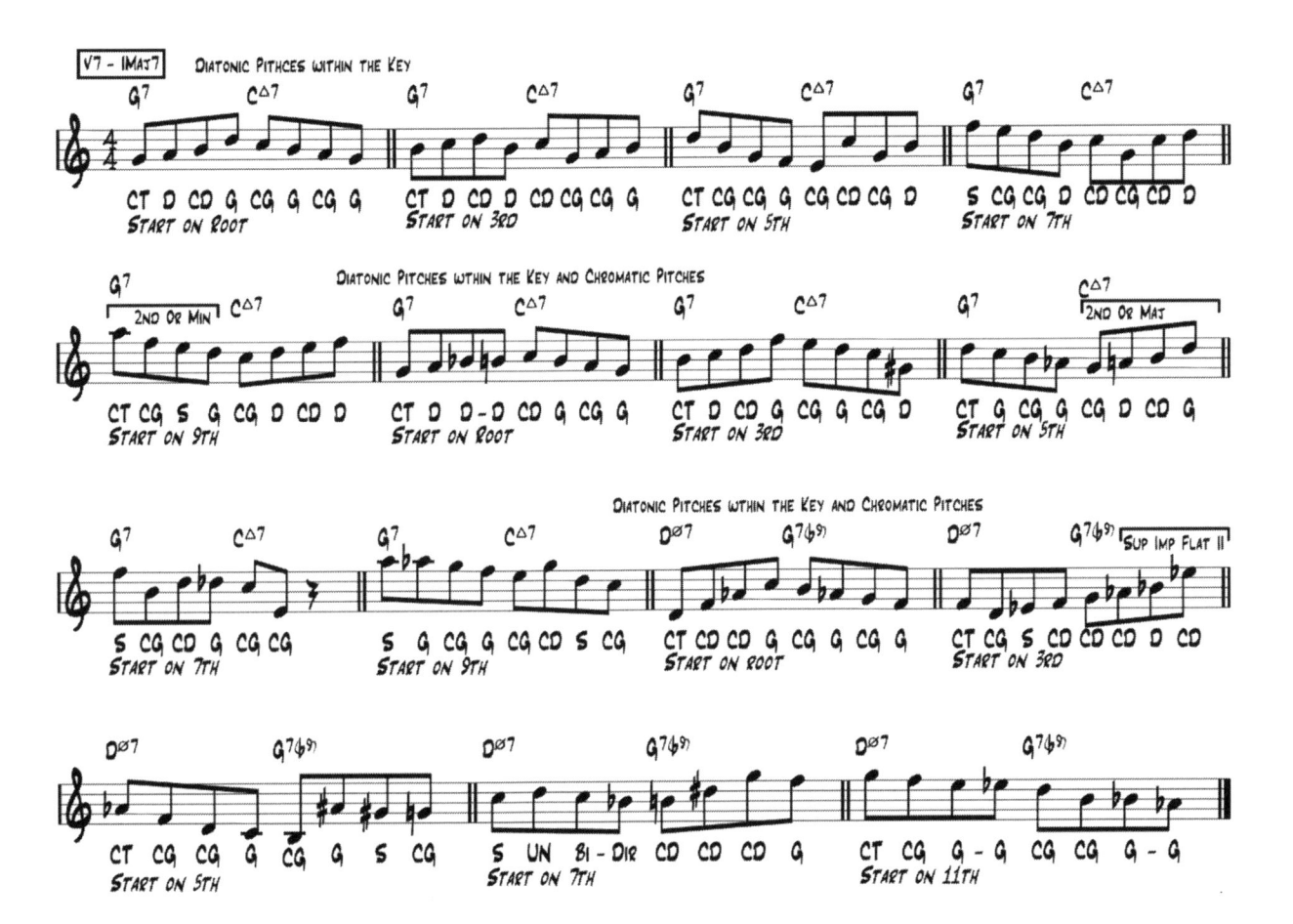

The Shape Method – Appendix III

Made in the USA
San Bernardino, CA
05 December 2014